Going Tradigital

Social Media Made Easy for Insurance Agents

Nadeem Damani

Angela Johnson

TEXAS RHINO PUBLISHING, LLC

Going Tra*digital*: Social Media Made Easy for Insurance Agents

ISBN: 978-0-9893486-0-7

Texas Rhino Publishing

Cover Design and Interior Layout: www.taylorbydesign.com

Dedication

For my daughter Aricka, who makes me want to be a better person. For my husband Ray, who with tremendous grace and love accepts my addiction to working. For my parents, sister, brother-in-law and precious nephew, you make my life so happy. For my grandparents, aunts, uncles, cousins and friends, who surround me with unconditional love and encouragement.I am blessed beyond measure.

— Angela

For my mother Nazlin, my first and my greatest teacher. For my dad, Nurudin, who opened my mind by introducing me to the world of books. For my loving wife Salima for all the support. For my sister Nadia for always being there for me and for rest of my family for all the love and support.

— Nadeem

Contents

Foreword

I REMEMBER HOW EXCITED I WAS WHEN I PURCHASED MY first personal computer in 1986. It was a Compaq 286 with a 5.25 floppy drive and 1 megabyte of memory! I majored in Computer Information Systems and used, even built, computers before—but this one was mine and I couldn't wait to open the huge box, put it together, and connect to the World Wide Web. That night, it took my wife forever to get off of the phone so I could connect. But when I finally did…Ah, the sound of the computer connecting to the Prodigy on-line service. It seems like only yesterday!

My friends couldn't understand why I would spend $2,000 (over two months' income) on a personal computer because back then, computers were considered to be only for business use. I found myself explaining to people on a regular basis what I actually used it for and even had a boss tell me that he believed personal computers were a fad that would soon disappear. I thought he was so old and outdated. I loved being on the cutting edge of technology and known as the guy who understood where it was all going. Technology of course changed at a rapid pace. It seemed that as soon as you got your computer home and took it out of the box another, faster processor was developed or a larger hard drive was created.

And here we are today over twenty-five years later. But instead of being the one with all of the answers and understanding where everything is going, I'm the old man who thought social networking was for kids and Facebook was just another sophisticated gossip board. Somehow, without me realizing it, I went to sleep and woke-up as a technologically challenged ex-computer nerd who couldn't tell the difference between a hashtag from an Instagram.

Over the past ten years I have spoken about, written about, and often publically criticized insurance agents who relied on technology to run their business. In the insurance industry, I felt the technology weakened the relationship between the agent and the customer and if we were going to survive, we had to get back to the basics, get out of the office and go see our clients. Although I continue to believe this today, I had no idea how using social media could improve relationship selling; that was until I met Angela Johnson and Nadeem Damani. They helped me understand that social media is simply a way to use technology as a means to a most traditional end: to develop stronger relationships with our clients.

When Angela and Nadeem asked me to write the Foreword for *Going Tradigital*, I was sincerely honored. For those of you who have not had the pleasure of meeting them, I can tell you from personal experience how both have always stayed on the cutting edge of technology and have found a way to bridge the gap between technology and relationship selling to grow two of the most successful Farmers Insurance agencies in the nation.

This book is not just about social marketing or networking—it's about using social media to better target your customers, find out who they are and why they buy, get more referrals, improve relationships and show them what makes your business different than everyone else's. They showed me the power of social media and the possibilities to use avenues such as Facebook, Twitter and YouTube to reach an audience of thousands, if not millions, to create a buzz about my business which can potentially bring my agency more customers than we ever dreamed possible. They can do that for you, too.

Although I found myself behind the curve when it comes to using social media, the good news is it's not too late for me, and it's not too late for you! Using the techniques mentioned in their book, you will undoubtedly increase sales, improve retention and build a stronger relationship with your customers who you are privileged to serve.

Going Tra*digital* may be an easy, fun read, but the message is powerful. I'll be buying a copy for every one of my employees and agents in my district and if you don't want to be left behind, I encourage you to do the same. Thank you Angela and Nadeem for showing this technologically challenged old man the light and for putting together a User's Guide without the complicated techie jargon.

@AngelaAJJohnson @nadeemd I wish U both continued success! #Tra*digital*.

Jeff Hastings
Farmers Insurance District Manager of the Year - 2005
EMyth Certified Business Coach

Jeff Hastings is the author of:

Recruit, Recruit, Recruit — How to Achieve Success One Agent at a Time

So You Want to be an Insurance Agent — A Step-By-Step Approach to a Successful Insurance Agency

So You Want to Own a Small Business (Available in the Winter 2013)

www.JeffHastingsAgency.com

www.twitter.com/BetterBizCoach

www.linkedin.com/In/JeffLHastings

www.facebook.com/FarmersCareerCenter

coach.emyth.com/jeffhastings

Introduction

"Social media won't make you young. But letting the world leave you behind is what makes you old."

—Michelle Shih

THE INTERNET HAS CHANGED ABSOLUTELY *EVERYTHING* IN the last two decades. There isn't one industry that has not been touched by the advances of the World Wide Web, and not one person who doesn't benefit from the conveniences it has to offer.

You may have heard the famous quote from Lao Tzu that 'A journey of a thousand miles begins with a single step.' Well the updated version of that is 'A journey of a thousand sites begins with a single click.'

Or how about the proverb, 'Give a man a fish and you feed him for a day. Teach a man to fish and you feed him for a lifetime.' Nowadays it's more appropriate to say, 'Give a person a fish and you feed him for a day; teach a person to use the Net and he won't bother you for weeks.'

We hope that made you LOL (laugh out loud), but you may be starting to wonder what all this has to do with selling insurance. Because insurance coverage is a legal requirement enforced by individual states, vehicle lenders and mortgage companies, we as agents have something that most other businesses crave—a captive audience.

However, we'd be willing to bet that many of you got into the insurance business not quite realizing how difficult it can be to succeed. It's not because there aren't enough prospects out there but because there are so many agents and direct writers competing for the same clients; clients who need a compelling reason to change insurance companies before agreeing to do so.

The most compelling reason for prospects to move their business to a different company is value. But how do we help them understand our value as an agent, or the value of the coverage our products offer? If they don't understand that critical value, they can easily be tempted to switch carriers by the offer of a lower rate.

As consumers, we all make decisions based on value every day. For instance, when purchasing clothing there is a vast difference in the quality and therefore, value, of items from Target and those sold at Nordstrom. The items sold at Target are less expensive but at Nordstrom, clients are assisted by a knowledgeable salesperson who recommends clothing that will fit better and last longer because the materials and construction are of a higher quality. Despite the large price gap between these two stores, Nordstrom has a dedicated clientele who see the value in their products and service, and are willing to pay more for that value.

The same goes for shoes. You wouldn't buy a pair of $20 athletic shoes from Payless if you are training for a marathon. Rather, you would pay more to go to a specialty running store where an experienced runner/salesperson will help you select a shoe that will provide the durability and stability to get you through the months of long training runs in comfort and style. The more expensive pair of running shoes will be lighter yet offer more cushioning. The protection and comfort the more expensive running shoes offers one's knees, shins and back is actually priceless and of a higher value to a runner.

Just like a Nordstrom sales associate, an insurance agent offers the protection and comfort of good value to his clients. It's a client saying that she trusts her agent because he's a real person who has devoted his career to his clients and community, has provided solid advice in the past, and genuinely cares about her future. In other words, she has a *relationship* with her agent. It's something she could be willing to pay a little more for, and that's highly instructive for all of us agents struggling to make ourselves known in this overcrowded market.

The good news is relationships are the name of the insurance game. It's not so much about who has the lowest premiums as it is about caring enough to learn about your clients—what they need and want, what they fear, and what products will provide the best value to properly protect their family and assets for the future.

Your interaction with clients and friends on social media can help create and strengthen client relationships like nothing ever has before! Throughout this book, you'll read stories of sales success that came directly from social media and find useful information on how you can duplicate that success.

For instance, how would you like to browse through your Facebook News Feed and see that a friend is shopping for home insurance? Or post a video about the value of life insurance only to earn $10,000 in commission the very next day from a family who watched that video and immediately called for an appointment?

Would you be interested in experiencing a double digit increase in retention? That can be possible when you use social media to deepen relationships and position your agency brand as a community leader in the minds of your clients.

These results can then be multiplied even further by having your staff use their social media networks to reach out to their connections as well. This will magnify the impact of your agency's social media presence.

That is happening every day for agents who are utilizing social media to interact with their community and it can happen for you, too.

The rise of the internet has brought new opportunities as well as new challenges for insurance agents. For instance, social media is a new marketing opportunity that has developed out of the growth and infiltration of the internet into our everyday lives. However, the growth of direct writers through the use of the internet has presented a new challenge for agents: the challenge to prove our value and worth to clients and prospects, and fight the direct writers' attempt to commoditize insurance.

Introduction

The time has come to turn the tables and win back our clients using the same technology that direct writers use to try to take away our clients. We need to change the game using the same weapon—the power of the internet. We can use social media to build one-on-one relationships with existing clients, as well as find new prospects to increase our book of business.

Direct writers can only use social media in a limited fashion. They can only have one Facebook page or one Twitter account for their brand. But a company with a large agency force can have *five, ten or twenty thousand* pages or more, one per agent. That can powerfully "humanize the brand," meaning the insurance company itself can be viewed for what it truly is, not a large faceless entity, but a business that is still based on individual service via a caring, knowledgeable, capable agency force.

Yes, the game is changing. Through social media you can reach people you never were able to even imagine contacting door-to-door—and at the same time, it allows you to have personal contact with all those potential clients who prefer to conduct their business online.

More and more agents are using social media to attract new clients, to keep existing clients and build relationships with clients at a deeper level. But many have shied away from using social media because they're scared of it or they don't understand it, or they've used it and it "didn't work."

That's why we wrote *Going* Tra*digital*. We coined the word tra*digital* because we believe the most successful insurance agents are those who use both traditional and digital touchpoints in their agencies. Have you ever heard the expression, "don't throw the baby out with the bathwater"? That's exactly our motto with *Going* Tra*digital*. You don't have to stop being a traditional agent. You can still do business in ways that you're comfortable and that many of your clients prefer too, which is face to face in the office or over the kitchen table.

But you can also integrate all the internet has to offer, both in your marketing and in your daily interactions with your current clients and prospects because there is now a large portion of consumers who are very comfortable connecting online.

We can remain a vibrant force in the minds of our clients and potential clients. It just takes some innovation, a willingness to try new things. By the end of this book, we hope that you are well on your way to incorporating social media into your marketing and customer retention strategies. But we also want you to keep this in mind—the vehicle for marketing and service may be changing, but the end goal of any interaction with our prospects or clients is still the same: an agent who cares.

What follows in *Going* Tra*digital* may challenge you, especially if you're not yet internet savvy, or if you have a Facebook account but you never used it or if you have only posted canned information. But if you stick with it and apply the techniques and suggestions we offer, you will learn how to integrate social media effectively into all that you are already doing as an agent. With social media bolstering your marketing efforts, you will be able to successfully execute the five elements of a growing insurance agency:

- Increase Prospecting and Opportunities for Sales
- Increase Customer Service
- Improve Retention and Cross Sales
- Gain Referrals
- Humanize Your Agency Brand

It doesn't matter how much time you've spent in the past on the internet. Our goal is to make this new medium for marketing totally accessible to you so that you can enjoy the success it can bring.

Most important, let us know how we're doing. Connect with us on Facebook at www.facebook.com/GoingTra*digital*. Tweet us at @goingtra*digital* or by using the hashtag #Tra*digital*. Join us in the global conversation, and in the meantime, you might be surprised at what your agency's phone starts to do once you begin integrating the traditional with the digital. Go Tra*digital*. And may your business never be the same again.

Sales and Marketing the Tra*digital* Way

> *"Your business is going to be cannibalized. The only question is who's going to do it—you or your competition."*
>
> —Steve Jobs

Do you recognize this?

You've acquired a list of prospects. You do what insurance agents have done since the advent of the telephone:

"Hello, Mrs. Smith. I'm Angela Johnson with Farmers Insurance—" and before you can say anything else, you hear that horrible, heart-sinking click.

Traditional Active Marketing

How many of you drive through a neighborhood and secretly wish that you could just knock on all those doors and introduce yourself? Door-to-door sales were tough, but what a great way to meet and get to know new prospects— for that magical price all agents like, free. Unfortunately, the only people who come to our door now are UPS drivers and the occasional local politician asking for a vote.

The good-old days of prospecting for business were tough but predictable. Insurance agents relied heavily on door-to-door sales and cold calling. The insurance, vacuum cleaner and encyclopedia door-to-door salesmen counted on housewives being home to not only answer the door but to have the time to listen to their sales pitch. But when women started entering the workforce in the mid- to late- twentieth century, fewer prospects were home to answer the door.

Additionally, because fewer women were home to keep a watchful eye on the neighborhood, restrictive city ordinances were put in place and that further shut the door on door-to-door sales. It turns out people don't want random salesmen, or criminals posing as salesmen, roaming their neighborhood during the day when no one is home. Go figure!

Cold calling took a hard hit with the Do Not Call Legislation. And if we really took a look at it, no one really ever liked being called at home. In the evening. At dinner time.

Many strong insurance agencies were built on cold calling and it might still be a viable way of prospecting if you call businesses, or call home phones and can get past the Do Not Call restriction, find the decision maker at home and get him or her interested in talking to you.

The reality is, cold calling is in its death throes if you think of the large numbers of households who have gotten rid of their home phone lines and opted to use VoIP or cell phones.

Angela worked for AT&T for many years, and this is what she discovered: In 2009, an average of one in four households, 24.5 percent, had ditched their home phone and gone totally wireless. This is up significantly from 2003 when that number was less than 5 percent. This number is much higher for those ages twenty-five to twenty-nine where 48.6 percent didn't have a home phone line![1]

Come to find out, the phone companies are experiencing some of the same issues we insurance agents are: they risk being crowded out by technology if they don't adapt. According to an AT&T FCC filing December 21, 2009, "Revenues from (home phone lines) are plummeting as customers cut their land lines in favor of the convenience and advanced features of wireless and VoIP services," the filing says. "Due to the high fixed costs of providing (land lines), every customer who abandons this service raises the average cost per line to serve the remaining customers." [2]

We have never looked at it that way, but it makes sense. The cost to maintain the old copper land lines is very expensive because it requires highly trained (and highly paid!) phone technicians, managers, and equipment on the ground in every city. Worse, phone companies are required by the FCC to maintain this infrastructure. As customers cancel their phone service, the only thing to do is shift this increasing cost to a smaller pool of customers.

That rising cost will eventually push most customers to get rid of their land line, which will raise the price for those who keep their home phones, which will make more people

[1] Don Reisinger. "CDC: One In four U.S. Homes Ditch Landlines. CNET.com. 13 May, 2010. http://news.cnet.com/8301-13506_3-20004885-17.html) . 12 December 2012.

[2] Jeff Bishop. "Telephone 'Land Lines' Obsolete?" Times-Herald.com Jan 05, 2010, (http://www.times-herald.com/local/Telephone-land-lines-obsolete-943949). 12 December, 2012.

get rid of them, and on and on until a land line phone at home is a thing of the past.

Hmmm, sounds a lot like what insurance companies do, doesn't it—using price to encourage customers to switch to a different product?

Fortunately for us, there is an inherent lie in the idea that technology is killing the traditional. People still need phones, but they want to use their cell phone instead of a landline. People still need to be able to communicate with *someone* to find the best insurance product for them. People still like to be referred to someone they know, like, and trust. It's just that the way that's done in the twenty-first century isn't over the phone or on someone's front porch anymore. The end result is still the same—connecting to potential and actual customers, but the way it's done is changing. Now, it can be done online.

Traditional Passive Marketing

Once you start looking at the problem of marketing, prospecting, and sales as still presenting the same problems but the way in which they're being done has changed, you start to see a pattern emerge. To illustrate this point, let's take two traditional passive forms of marketing: the phone book and T.V. commercials.

Passive marketing consists of building a platform and relying on prospects to find you and/or take action to contact you. Advertising in a phone book goes something like this: An Insurance Agent pays (a lot of) money for ad space in the yellow pages with the idea that when people need a service they will go to the phone book. The agency's ad creativity makes the agency stand out from the other insurance agent listings, and the hope is that the shopper will be compelled to call the Agent who placed the ad. It is a great idea, and this strategy worked very well for a long time. We, like you, grew up pulling out the phone book to look up business information. If you needed more information, like hours of operation or directions, you just called the phone number and asked. Awesome!

Unfortunately, the Yellow Pages always had inherent drawbacks. You could call columns of numbers and find that maybe 25 percent of the listings were out of date. Whether the business had moved, gone out of business or just changed phone numbers, it was always a labor-intensive way to select a service provider. Using static information that is only updated only once a year just doesn't cut it anymore, and thus the phone book is no longer the most viable way for people to find you—but people still need insurance agents and they still need to be able to find you. They can do so very easily on the internet.

Then there's the marketing vehicle no one could ever imagine becoming obsolete, perhaps the greatest invention of the twentieth century, the television. T.V. commercials created a revolutionary method to get a marketing message out to vast groups of people at one time. Commercials allowed marketers to humanize their brand in a way print advertising couldn't. By singing catchy jingles and presenting attractive images, commercials quickly became part of our everyday lives.

Even commercials, however, are being squeezed out. With the invention of things like TiVo and the DVR, we can now digitally record our favorite TV shows and watch them later, commercial free. As we fast forward through commercials we think, "Ahhh. Isn't this nice? No one yelling at me to go buy a car! No waiting for two minutes to find out what happens next. *No Commercials.*" How wonderful, except if you're the one doing the advertising, because now suddenly you don't have an audience!

But always remember, people still need information and it is vital to find a way to communicate with potential clients. Of course, both phone books and T.V. commercials have been pushed aside by the ever-present and ever-expanding technology offered by computers and the internet. Consumers are now able to get all the business names, addresses and phone numbers they need on the Internet thru company web sites and social media pages.

Business web sites and social media pages provide much more specific information to shoppers than commercials can; important information to the consumer such as hours of operation, business specialties and culture, information on staff, and detailed information on what sets each business apart from their competitors.

In other words, agents and their specific agencies still need a way to get their message out—that's always going to be the case, just as people are always going to need insurance. That's the traditional aspect of this business that will never change.

But the hard reality is, with the internet, consumers have become accustomed to more. They want more information, they want it faster, and most important, they want to feel as if they can connect with you in a more immediate way—not just an occasional phone call during business hours. And here's the rub with traditional forms of marketing and advertising: the consumer can't interact with a commercial, they can't ask questions of a print ad, they're unable to ask a radio commercial for a new quote.

When large insurance companies create these types of one-way advertising, all we as agents can do is sit back and hope that it drives business to our individual offices through brand-name recognition.

But not all agents are alike and not all agencies offer the same benefits. Although agents who represent the same carriers certainly offer the same product, each agency has a different value proposition. There are as many agency environments as there are agents.

So how do you market the value proposition of your agency and tell prospects and clients what sets you apart from every other XYZ company agent out there? By using a different medium to get the same message out.

Our potential customers have grown accustomed to gathering lots of information in order to make the best buying decision for themselves and their families. They want more information, more research, more cost comparisons and in the insurance world, more product, company, and agency comparisons. Because almost everyone has access to the Internet, many consumers are conducting this research online. That can be bad news because that leaves them open to finding their way to a competitor.

All-Important Customer Service

However, there is also good news: research also shows that despite researching insurance options online, consumers still prefer to seek out a local agent when they are ready to purchase insurance. Why is this good news? Because we now have social media.

In a wonderful twist of fate, social media has humanized the buyer/seller relationship. People have grown to like the connection that they can get with someone on Facebook. They also expect higher and higher levels of availability from the businesses they use. In short, customers are demanding a higher-level of customer service and social media makes that easy.

It's an advantage that the Internet has given all insurance agents, if we choose to look at it that way. To do that requires a little shift in our traditional thinking. A Monday thru Friday 9:00 a.m. to 5:00 p.m. schedule used to be enough for an insurance office, but that is not the case anymore.

As the Internet advances and infiltrates every part of our society, clients expect to have access to us 24/7. That's physically impossible, and while more brick and mortar businesses are extending their hours of operation, many of us have figured out that implementing a strong online presence makes good business sense because it is convenient for our customers.

In the article, "Social Media Branding Strategy: Using 'Touch Points' to Create Strong Brands," Dean Hambleton explains it this way:

Scale and platform has changed how people, especially people in a global economy, communicate. In new media, brands are created when one person communicates to another person, usually their friend about a product and its benefits. 'Friends' have a conversation and brands are recommended. This recommendation among friends creates world class brands. Social media has evolved modern marketing from a 'push' world, in which products are produced and pushed on consumers to a 'pull' world in which consumers dictate to marketers what the consumer wants.[3]

If there is anything "new" in the world of insurance, it is exactly what Hambleton is alluding to, shifting customer service expectations. As technology progresses and businesses offer more personalized, faster customer service, our insurance clientele are beginning to expect elevated customer service from our agencies as well.

Consider this: Many years ago when a customer called to order a pizza for delivery, they would tell the employee their name and address, maybe ask what the specials are and then place their order. Today a consumer can order a pizza multiple ways. They can go online and enter their login information which then triggers the system to pull up their last order or maybe their favorite pizza. They select the items they want (down to whether they prefer light or heavy sauce), select a delivery time and click "Submit." They don't have to go get their wallet and enter payment information because the system stored their credit card information the last time they ordered. In thirty minutes, *voilá,* a pizza delivery guy is knocking on the door.

[3] Dean Hambelton. "Social media Branding Strategy: Using 'Touch Points' to Create Strong Brands. EzineArticles.com. March 29, 2011. http://EzineArticles.com/6127432. January 5, 2013.

Or the customer may call the store directly, but instead of having to give all their contact information to the employee, the guy or girl already knows who it is. The employee greets the customer by name and asks the customer if they'll be having their usual order. It's kind of simple if you think about it. The pizza joint uses software that stores phone numbers, names, addresses, orders and payment information.

And that gives us something to think about. When someone gets that level of service for a $20 pizza, how much more should they expect from us as agents who they pay $500 to $1000 per month? When others are raising the bar, we have to lead, follow, or get out of the way.

Buying insurance isn't the same as buying a pizza. There is no tangible product for that matter. The largest value proposition an agency can offer that sets them apart from others is, and always has been, customer service. Where product and price are the same among agents representing the same company, service and convenience is the only distinguishing factor.

Unfortunately, too many agents are resisting change, are fighting transitioning their business to one that incorporates, fundamentally, the advantages the internet has to offer, and thus they risk falling so far behind it will be difficult, if not impossible, to catch up.

Borders bookstore is a great, yet sad, example of a company that didn't react to a changing marketplace. Founded in 1971 by brothers Tom and Louis Borders, it was a very successful company across the United States. Their first international store was opened in Singapore in

1997. In 2003, they operated 1,249 stores under the Borders and Waldenbooks brand and in 2004 Borders reached an agreement with Seattle's Best Coffee to operate cafes in its domestic superstores. All seemed to be going well. Borders expanded their business slowly and methodically. They seemed to be thriving but when the end came, it came quickly.

During the rise of the internet Borders opened an online store, but they didn't invest the time or resources into it they should have. They failed to see the impact the internet would have on business.

In 2001, as their online store struggled, it was viewed as a distraction from the core bricks and mortar retail business. Borders made the decision to outsource their e-commerce to Amazon.com. Short term, it was convenient. Long term, it was fatal, as Borders never took the necessary steps to transform the organization so that digital would become a true core competence of their business.

The last time Borders made a profit was 2006. Its yearly income dropped by $1 billion over the next four years. They closed all stores in 2011.

Compare this to Amazon.com. The website went online in 1995, and it attracts sixty-five million customers to its U.S. web site *monthly*. People love the convenience of shopping from home.

In November 2007, Amazon led the market when they launched Kindle, a low priced tool eReader that encourages customers to buy more books. Brilliant! During Q3 2010, e-book sales for its Kindle reader outnumbered sales of hardcover books. Amazon claims that, during that period, 180 e-books were sold for every 100 hardcover books. They saw the eReader trend and have capitalized on it.

Amazon is nothing more than a search engine if you think about it, but they've made their customers feel so welcome. You can submit reviews, not just read them. You can feel like you're picking up the book, just like in a brick and mortal store, with the 'Search Inside' feature. The website is also "smart," suggesting books based on your previous purchases, which further personalizes the shopping experience. Customers are experiencing this level of convenience and service in other industries as well and are beginning to expect it from the insurance industry.

The moral of these two tales should be clear: instead of groaning under the weight of it all and going the way of Borders, we can be innovative like Amazon. We, too, can hold on to and even expand our market share.

As professional insurance agents, we all believe that a strong insurance plan is critical to protecting the assets of individuals and families. Whether you are a life, health, personal lines or commercial agent, the customized protection we offer provides benefits that most consumers don't fully realize they need. That is, until they need them.

Because direct writers utilize the Internet and/or call center business model, the only way they can gain customers is to make people believe they don't need personalized advice and that price is the only thing that separates one company from another. Their message is that all you need to do is call an 800-number or go online and get a policy started.

Daily, they are pushing and pushing consumers to believe that insurance is a commodity and that price is all that matters; in other words, the advice of an insurance agent is irrelevant. They lead consumers to believe they don't need the advice or expertise of a professional insurance agent.

Some days, when someone brings in a new ID card from an internet insurance company and wants to cancel their auto policy, it sure does feel like the push to commoditize insurance is working.

The Agent as Trusted Professional

Our challenge is to position ourselves as a trusted professional in the minds of our clients in order to retain and grow our businesses. It goes back, time and again, to good-old customer service, and this is where we can really excel if we are willing to try some new things.

Many agents today still operate with a Monday through Friday, 9:00 a.m. to 5:00 p.m. office schedule. If someone calls the office on Friday at 5:15 p.m., they must wait until Monday at 9:00 a.m. for a return call. In those instances, clients are inconvenienced when they can't reach someone after hours or on the weekends.

A few years ago, this wasn't a big issue. Very few, if any, consumers could reach their agent's office after hours so this was an acceptable level of service. That just isn't the case today. There are plenty of insurance companies that are call center based and can provide answers online or by phone 24/7. Consumers are beginning to expect to be able to interact with their service providers according to *their* channel of preference, not the agent's.

This is where social media becomes your most powerful weapon. With Facebook, Twitter and LinkedIn accounts growing exponentially every day, your customers can connect with you via these social media sites. They know it. They love it, and with it, you can make this push for convenience your ally.

Social media has all sorts of misconceptions attached to it. There are some agents who understand that social media and digital branding is important but they aren't sure how to implement an effective strategy. Other agents have tried setting up a Facebook or LinkedIn account but aren't getting the results they desire.

We have been there and we understand. Using social media is different from any other form of advertising or marketing you have ever seen or tried. Wait, that's not exactly true. Once you come to understand social media and how to use it effectively, you're going to find that it's the digital replacement for door-to-door sales and cold calling because it's a lot like face-to-face networking.

Social media gives you access to potentially thousands of new prospects, just like a T.V. ad, and it is acts like the Yellow Pages on steroids, because people can easily find you and instead of an expensive ad that looks just like every other ad in print, on Facebook or Linked in, you can let your individuality shine through.

We're the first to admit it. Figuring out how to harness the incredible power social media offers isn't always easy. We have made our share of mistakes. We have accidentally found social media strategies that work. We have done our due diligence and have slogged through the research. Through it all, we have honed our social media skills.

At one point several years ago, many thought that social media would never supplant traditional forms of marketing. They were wrong. Social media allows us to do everything the traditional forms of marketing once did—letting people know who we are, finding new prospects, but because it personalizes the whole transaction on line, it gives us something the traditional never could: more access and wider spheres of influence.

Please allow us to show you what we have learned so you don't have to make the same mistakes we did. Our goal is to have you enjoying the fruits of social media far quicker than we did.

2   The Tra*digital* Agent and Agency

> *"What the wise man does in the beginning, the fool does in the end."*
>
> —Warren Buffett

WE HOPE BY NOW YOU REALIZE THAT IN THIS NEW AGE OF social media, it is imperative to have an online presence so that clients and prospects can easily find and communicate with you. Now more than ever, our clients and prospects are working and playing online, and they need to find our agencies there as well.

We want to be very clear about something. We aren't suggesting that you close your brick and mortar office and launch an online-only agency. We aren't suggesting that you drop all of your traditional marketing methods and use social media alone. What we are suggesting is that you create a tra*digital* agency and become a tra*digital* agent. This will require you to enhance your existing **traditional** agency by deploying a combination of online ***digital*** initiatives to capture new business, increase agency efficiency and improve customer satisfaction.

Tra*digital* Agency Defined

What do we mean by a tra*digital* agent/agency? We defined tra*digital* in the introduction as combining traditional with digital. Specifically that means bringing together the best of both worlds offline and online to create a stronger, more robust agency. It's a hybrid, that which results when two things are blended so that the best characteristic of each item is brought together into a finished product.

Many of you may have a hybrid bicycle, which is a blend of a sturdy mountain bike combined with the speed of a road bike. And perhaps the most popular hybrid of all is the hybrid vehicle, which uses two or more "distinct power sources to move the vehicle." [4]

A tra*digital* agency, then, is one that has both a "clicks and bricks" presence. "Clicks" refers to the ability clients and prospects have to find and initiate business with you online, and "bricks" represents a traditional office storefront where people who prefer can do business with you in person. Just like a hybrid vehicle, a tra*digital* agency uses two or more distinct sources to power the agency. Wouldn't it be great to know you're powering your agency from multiple sources?

Clicks + Bricks = Powerful Agency Advantage

We know what you're thinking. You, like us, pay money each month to buy or lease an office and are required to cover all of the expenses that go along with maintaining that brick and mortar presence: electricity, cleaning service, phone system and the other necessary costs of doing business. It's the main reason why many of us have

---

[4] All definitions taken from Wikipedia. http://en.wikipedia.org/wiki/Hybrid_bicycle; http://en.wikipedia.org/wiki/Hybrid_car

been so reluctant to admit that consumers are doing their shopping online.

You may also be thinking that consumers are passing us by, and we as agents are eventually doomed to failure in our clean, expensive brick and mortar offices. Or perhaps you're thinking that you don't need to change anything. You would prefer to just plug along and run a traditional brick and mortar agency with no social or digital engagement.

Please don't make the mistake Borders did. Don't shut down on us yet! Keep your mind open because the good stuff is coming.

Thad Rueter, in an article for InternetRetailer.com says that a survey conducted by PwC found that *83 percent* of US consumers go online for research before buying products and services *from brick and mortar stores*. This same survey also found that 32 percent of US consumers follow brands online. As customers become more Internet savvy, they are using online resources to gather product information, read reviews and see what friends are saying about the brand on social media.

Rueter goes on to say, "…Most consumers continue to shop across different channels, which include the web, physical stores, catalogs, TV shopping networks and mobile. Eighty-six percent of all respondents, and 65 percent of those in the United States, shop across at least two channels, the report says. Twenty-one percent of global respondents, and 25 percent of U.S. consumers, shop across at least four." Your clients and prospects are comparison shopping, not only for price but for convenience. In fact, in this same survey they found " … that the convenience of online shopping (cited by 28 percent of respondents) beat out low prices (25 percent) as the main reason consumers are attracted to web merchants."[5] So what do you think will happen if prospects are looking online to comparison shop and they never even find information about your agency? That answer is easy. You won't even be a factor in their decision-making process because they won't know you exist, which means you are too difficult (and inconvenient) to do business with. Your agency won't be given a chance to compete for that business.

If you're thinking, "so what, the Reuter article is primarily referring to retail products," think again. The same shopping behavior has been found to be true for insurance sales as well. In his article written for Insurance and Financial Advisor magazine, Bob Graham states, "The majority of insurance sales begin online, but most are still completed by insurance agents…"[6] No matter how convenient the search for insurance is online, nothing can replace the advice of a licensed insurance agent.

If your agency is anything like ours, you have people constantly calling for quotes because their current policy suffers from insufficient coverages. These prospects have come to realize that their current insurance has lots of gaps and holes that could destroy them financially.

---

[5] Thad Reuter. "Most Shoppers Go Online to Research Products Before Buying In Stores." InternetRetailer.com. March 30, 2012. http://www.internetretailer.com/2012/03/30/most-shoppers-go-online-research-products. December, 15, 2012.

[6] Bob Graham. "Online sales of insurance rising; agents still playing major role." IFAwebnews.com. June 20, 2012. http://ifawebnews.com/2012/06/20/online-sales-of-insurance-rising-agents-still-playing-major-role/

Do you know what's interesting? We frequently ask the simple question, "Who recommended these coverages?" and people almost always reply, "I chose these myself with an online company."

As we go about the routine of explaining the coverages they are missing and providing scenarios of what can happen without those coverages, or explaining what the limits of liability mean, we close that sale at least 85–90 percent of the time, even if we don't beat the price. The client is so disturbed by the uninformed choices they made and the implications those decisions could have had on their family, they want to correct the mistakes right away.

The average consumer still prefers to have a traditional agent they can meet for completing the sale and on whom they can rely for future advice and assistance. The client still wants to know they have a live, local person whose professional wisdom they can count on. Insurance consumers, much like retail consumers, are arming themselves with information online; yet they still seek guidance from a professional.

It's no surprise, then, that agencies that are able to initiate and capture sales online *and* offline, and are able to provide service via social media or other technology *or* in person at a local office—a tra*digital* agent in other words—will have the highest chance of success.

Remaining Relevant in an Online World

The critical issue for us as insurance agents in this rapidly changing marketing environment is to remain relevant. If recent television marketing campaigns are any indication, insurance companies are attempting to lighten the image of insurance as a whole. Instead of being seen as cautious and conservative, agents are caring supportive friends, there to help when help is needed.

All major insurance companies are using advertising to reach out to the public in new and creative ways. However, this book isn't about what the brand(s) you represent is doing to stay current. It is about helping all of us, the agents, remain relevant in a competitive marketplace as more and more people are choosing to conduct some, most or all of their day-to-day business online.

Let's take two examples of traditional ways of thinking about brick-and-mortar business and look at it through the social media lens.

Location, Location, Location!

Location, Location, Location. When you hear that, what do you think of? This one word repeated three times is synonymous with the ability of a business to fail or succeed simply based on where it is located. Here are common considerations when choosing a brick-and-mortar store front:

- Visibility is the primary consideration when selecting a location for an agency. If people driving down the street can't see our business, they will not be inclined to visit our agency. A highly visible location is an indicator of our future ability to succeed.

- Accessibility is another important factor in determining a profitable location. When a business is difficult to access because of high traffic, odd or no turning lanes, bad parking or dim lighting, potential clients will drive down the road to an agency that is easier to access.

- Suitability must be considered when looking for an agency location as well. As an agent, we want to make sure our products are suitable for the area residents and that the location we select is in an area where we will want to spend our time.

However, just as social media is simply a new medium in which to do traditional insurance marketing and sales, social media mimics the very best of brick and mortar placement. To prove our point, let's look at this same list with a view towards social media:

- Visibility—Just as physical visibility is important for our brick and mortar location, in today's digital age it is critical that your agency is visible online. If people searching for insurance online don't see our business, they will not do business with our agency. A highly visible Tra*digital* agency is an indicator of future ability to succeed.

- Accessibility is another important factor in determining a profitable agency. When an agency is difficult to communicate with, prospects will move on down the digital road to a Tra*digital* agency that is accessible online.

- Suitability must be considered when determining which social media platforms to use. As agents, we want to make sure our products and message are suitable for the platform(s) and that it is a network where we will want to spend our time.

It's no coincidence that the top three factors of visibility, accessibility and suitability when selecting a physical location also perfectly describe the reasons our agencies need to have an online presence. It follows the same pattern as land-lines giving way to cell phones: the need is still there; the solution is different.

Where The People Are

As successful business owners, we know we must go where the prospects and clients are in order to remain relevant. Traditional thinking tells us that if you are a P&C agent, you need to put yourself either directly in front of homeowners or renters, or people who deal with homeowners or renters, like realtors or property management companies.

How many times do you see people, grown adults no less, walking down the street or sitting in a restaurant with their heads buried in their smartphones? How often do you start to tell someone a story and they interrupt you by saying, "Yes, I saw that on Facebook"?

If Angela wants to get in touch with her daughter, she has to send her a Tweet. To quickly contact his parents, Nadeem has to post on their Facebook wall. Even email has become almost obsolete for quick touch points with family and friends. If we want to connect with someone who prefers online engagement in a meaningful way, social media is the place to do it.

It's like Angela told one of her agent friends who just couldn't understand why she needed to be online. Angela said point blank: If you're not online, then I have no idea you even exist. If you aren't managing an active presence on social media sites, you are giving your leads and opportunities to the agents who do have an engaging online presence.

According to a Pew Research survey published in August, 2011, 65 percent of adult internet users now say they use a social networking site. Not only are they using social media to connect with family and friends, these consumers are turning to social media more and more frequently to find products and services, or even more important, *to ask their family and friends* about products and services.

When on networking sites, it is very easy to see when your friend likes/follows/comments about a product or service. Therefore, as a business owner, our reach is extended beyond just our immediate connections. It is expanded by reaching the friends of our connections, thereby creating a virtual referral network.

Above all, don't make assumptions about social media. One of the fastest growing demographics on Facebook is people over fifty. A recent report, *Demographics of Internet Users*, notes that baby boomers and seniors are steadily *increasing their use* of the Internet. Seventy-seven percent of those aged fifty to sixty are online; and 54 percent of those aged sixty-five and older are using the Internet.[7] According to Aiden Hijleh, seniors are "more likely to stay on our pages longer and thoroughly review and absorb the information provided."[8]

So the facts are clear. Consumers are online more than ever before so this is where we need to be engaged. To stay

---

[7] Kathryn Zickuhr and Mary Madden. Pew Internet and American Life Project. www.PewInternet.org. June 6, 2012. http://www.pewinternet.org/Reports/2012/Older-adults-and-internet-use.aspx. Jan 7, 2013.

[8] Aiden Hijleh. "How To Appeal To Facebook's Fastest Growing Demographic: Seniors. Allfacebook.com. October 4, 2011. http://allfacebook.com/facebook-seniors_b61114. January 6, 2013

in business, we need to go where our potential customers are. That's no longer solely the retail shopping center or office building. We have our offices in which we run our day-to-day operations, but incorporating social media into those operations is vital if we want to keep growing our business and be a success.

Success has always meant that insurance agents either remain or become the logical choice in the mind of the consumer. This traditionally happened through things such as community presence and newspaper advertising. However, since our clients are online, we need to be there too. In order to remain relevant, we have to either begin utilizing social media or retool the effectiveness of our online presence, and that's what the rest of this book is all about.

3

How to Set-up and Grow Your Social Networks

"Action without planning is the cause of all failure. Action with planning is the cause of all success."

—Brian Tracy

WE HOPE BY NOW YOU UNDERSTAND THE NECESSITY OF building an online presence, but not at the expense of what has traditionally worked for you in the past. In order to be successful with social media, it is a good idea to start at the beginning—by simply setting up your social media account(s) correctly.

If our research showed us anything, it illustrated that if a user didn't set up their social media accounts correctly from the get go, then ineffectiveness was sure to follow. Utilizing social media as a marketing tool in an agency requires some dedicated time to set up accounts in an organized, professional manner.

You need to do some basics, such as setting up your profile(s) and uploading contacts from your email list or CRM (customer relations management) software.

If you already have your social media accounts set up and running, you could easily skip some or all of this chapter—but you might find some of the information in the later parts of the chapter useful. Whatever the case, skim through and see what works for you.

Choosing Your Social Media Networks

Below is a list of some of the most popular social media networks that will get you the most bang for your buck and allow easy, meaningful connections with clients and prospects. We recommend starting with Facebook. However, if you deal exclusively with businesses, then you could start with LinkedIn.

We also recommend selecting just one platform to start, and then as you get comfortable, add one at a time into your processes so that you don't get overwhelmed. Facebook, LinkedIn, and Twitter are still considered the "big three" in social media, but YouTube (for video) and Pinterest (for pictures) are gaining in popularity.

Platform URLs

The following is simply a list of all the important social media URL's so you know where to go to get signed up:

Facebook Personal Profile — www.facebook.com
Facebook Business Page — www.facebook.com/pages/create.php
LinkedIn — www.linkedin.com
Google+ Local — plus.google.com/local
Twitter — www.twitter.com
Foursquare — www.foursquare.com

Yelp — www.yelp.com

Email Newsletter — www.constantcontact.com or www.mailchimp.com

YouTube — www.youtube.com

Pinterest — www.pinterest.com

Instagram — www.instagram.com

Getting Set Up on the Big Three

Now that you know where to find the networking sites, let's roll our sleeves up and get started using them. And that's the secret—just get started! Too many times people get stalled because they think they need to know more about something, or they're scared they are going to make a mistake and then it's all over. We suggest that as you read the following, put your book by your computer and "just do it," (as Nike reminds us all the time.)

The Basics of Facebook

You know how we call facial tissue "Kleenex" and plastic wrap, "Saran wrap." That's because those brands have become synonymous with the actual product. If there was an equivalent in the social media world, it would be Facebook. It is the most popular network with over 1.06 billion monthly active users. It is also the easiest to learn to use and the best place to find a wide range of people. This ensures that no matter what type of agent you are, you are likely to find a multitude of ideal client prospects at your fingertips!

First things first: A personal Facebook account is called a *profile*. A business Facebook account is called a *page*.

If you don't already have one, you will need to set up a personal Facebook profile first. Go to http://www.facebook.com. Create a username and password and follow the steps to create your personal Facebook profile. Be sure to completely fill in all of the information about yourself so more people can find you!

Once your personal profile is complete, go to https://www.facebook.com/pages/create.php to create your business page. You will likely want to select Company, Organization or Institution and then choose Insurance Company from the drop-down menu. Just continue following the steps along until your business page is complete.

Remember to completely fill in **all** of the information about your business so people can easily see how to contact or do business with you. There is nothing more frustrating than going to a business Facebook page and not being able to find out how to contact them with questions or buy something from them!

The reason we like Facebook is that it gives you the most bang for your buck. It is user-friendly and fairly intuitive to use. Once you set up your personal profile and business page and have used your contact list to start your network, you can start building your fresh "fans."

The Basics of Twitter

Twitter is an excellent place to connect with local centers of influence and many others who can help build your agency.

To sign up for Twitter go to: https://twitter.com/signup. Here you will enter your name and email address, then create a password and create a username. Your Twitter *username* is also called your Twitter "handle."

The Twitter handle you select is important. Since Twitter only allows 140 characters per message, a long username/handle will make it difficult for others to reply to you or to retweet your content. It should be short and descriptive, leaving the most characters possible for your actual message.

For instance, your first name and last initial is a great option. Nadeem's Twitter handle is @nadeemd. That's easy and short. As agents, we want clients and prospects to remember our names, not the name of the brand we sell. Social media is all about what makes us as agents unique, so try to select a Twitter handle that includes your name.

If you have a common name, like Angela Johnson, this can be difficult. Angela's twitter handle is @AngelaAJJohson. That is a little too long, but it was the best she could do and believe us, she tried a lot of names.

In the example below, someone named Joe Smith is also going to have a hard time selecting a unique but easy to remember Twitter handle. You can see that Twitter is recommending 'JoeSmit44937886'. That would be a bad choice! It's too long and complicated.

For all you common namers out there, we feel your pain. Just keep trying until you find a combination that will be easy for others to spell and remember.

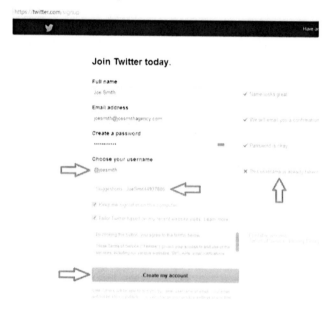

Just like on Facebook, Twitter allows a profile picture. This can be the same picture you used on your business Facebook page.

Twitter also has something similar to the Facebook cover photo, called a header. This is a way to visually describe yourself to your Twitter followers. Be sure to completely fill out your Twitter profile so your followers can easily contact you outside of Twitter.

Lastly, whatever you do, don't "protect" your business Twitter account by locking it. The whole idea of social media is to be social! Your professional Twitter account is a place where you want people to easily find and interact with you as a business. Creating a barrier to doing business with you is a huge turn-off in the social media world.

If you already have a Twitter account that is locked down, no worries. Just go into your account settings and uncheck the box that says Protect My Tweets. Be sure to click "Save Changes" at the bottom of the form to save your changes.

If you must lock an account, create a separate Twitter account and use that one to limit who can see your personal Tweets. Your professional Twitter account should always be public and unprotected.

The Basics of LinkedIn

To join LinkedIn, go to http://www.linkedin.com/join. You can enter your name, email address and select a password, or connect to LinkedIn using your Facebook account.

Once you have logged in, LinkedIn will walk you through the screens needed to set up your profile. LinkedIn is a very professional network and not the place for zany pictures or comments.

On LinkedIn you want to position yourself as an insurance professional and lay out your profile like a resume. Remember: Your profile is being looked at by prospects who are deciding if they should "hire" you as their professional insurance agent.

The more information you provide to LinkedIn in your profile, the more connections the system recommends for you. That's the key to success on LinkedIn where the name of the game is connections. This isn't the network to hold back information due to privacy concerns or fear of bragging.

For instance, it's not really an invasion of your privacy if you list the college you attended, is it? But this bit of information will allow LinkedIn to connect you with alumni who like to do business with others from their alma mater. Cha ching!

More Tips For Creating Social Media Profiles

Social media success first rests on creating an informative profile. The information above just walked you through the very basic steps of doing just that. But think about first impressions—they matter.

Also, it is vital to make sure your agency brand is consistent across all platforms you utilize. Ideally, people are going to be following you on multiple sites and so consistency becomes part of your agency brand.

Here are some suggestions for standardizing your personal agency brand. Some of this will come naturally (especially when you come to fully understand that on social media, being your genuine self is must) and some are just good reminders:

- For your business Facebook page, select a profile picture that you will use across all networks. People will begin to associate that picture with your agency.
- Facebook cover photos are fun. You can change them based on the season, awards and recognition you or your agency have received, promotions your agency is running or products you want to highlight.

- On Facebook, your personal and business profile pictures should be *different* so people can easily tell if you are commenting as yourself or representing your business. Trust us—it can get confusing when the same picture is used for both accounts.

- Twitter headers are meant to be fun. You can change them based on the season, awards and recognition you or your agency have received, promotions your agency is running or products you want to highlight.

- For social media networks that allow customization, select a basic color scheme and stick to it across all social media platforms, website and blog.

- Have a consistent tone and message in your posts and engagement with online friends.

- Create a standard agency description and save it to a file on your computer. Most social media platforms include a spot for a business description. While you can tweak this message slightly for each platform, your readers should get the same basic message about your agency no matter where they view it.

- Take some time to have each social media platform direct users to another one of your platforms, taking them deeper down the sales funnel each time and inching them closer to a sale.

- On your personal Facebook Profile, there is an "About" section. This section is where you will enter information about yourself. The information you enter in this section appears just below your profile picture on Facebook. It is very important that you list your agency as your Employer and link it to your Facebook Business Page. This allows your friends to easily find out how they can do business with you!

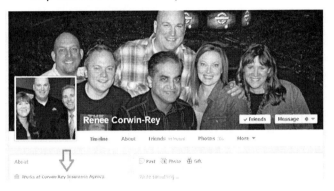

Building Contacts In Your Networks

Once you have created your profile(s), connecting with people is the next step regardless of which platform you choose to work with. Your social media success depends on developing an engaged audience for your posts and getting people interested in you as you become genuinely interested in them. That's when the good connections (the ones that can lead to new business) start to happen.

In the early days of social media (less than a decade ago!), you would have to painstakingly find people you knew or who you think might be interested in connecting with you. That is no longer the case.

Just like building any network, online or off, you connect first with people you know, and all the networks have made it very easy to do just that.

Your existing contacts are like a gold mine. These are your key contacts, friends, clients, family members and current and former co-workers. They know you well and will not hesitate to add you and may even feel complimented that you invited them to join your networks.

This can be done quickly and easily. Simply download a list of contacts into a workable Excel spreadsheet and then upload the contacts to the respective platform.

For example, for the Facebook business page there is an option to upload a contact list. Once it is uploaded, Facebook will send out invites to their email addresses and you've got some fans right away! Here's what the page looks like:

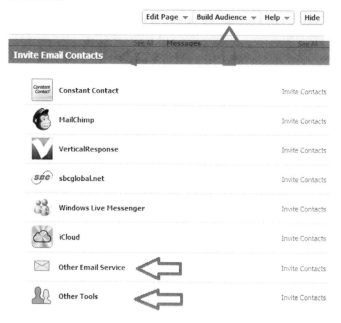

The same thing can be done with LinkedIn, see below.

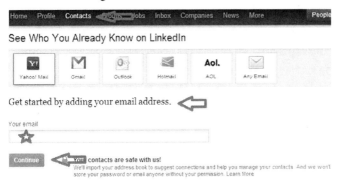

You can also easily connect with your existing contacts on Twitter. Here's how:

To look up contacts from your address book:

1. Go to the **Discover** page and click on **Find friends**.
2. Select **Search Contacts** next to your email provider (Gmail, Yahoo, etc).
3. **Enter your email log in credentials** when prompted. (Please make sure your browser enables pop ups!)
4. When asked if you agree to share your information with Twitter, click **Agree** or **Allow access**.
5. Contacts who are already on Twitter will be shown. Follow individuals by clicking **Follow**, or follow all contacts by clicking **Follow all**.
6. You can invite contacts to join Twitter from this page as well. We won't send an email automatically; you select who to invite from a list that appears after you click **Invite**.

If you use any other CRM software like ACT or if your company has its own proprietary database software, you can download your book of business into an Excel spreadsheet and repeat the same process. This gives you instant connections with your existing clients.

We have found that once we're connected to friends and clients on social media, they will start introducing us to old friends and contacts we may have lost touch with. When you start posting pictures and other content, their friends will notice you and make comments. You may realize they are familiar to you. You may find that you like what they say, and you may decide to add them to your Facebook network.

Or those friends, acquaintances and clients who come in contact with you through your posts from their friends, acquaintances, and clients, may like what they see and ask you to "friend" them. That's the essence of networking, and it doesn't matter if you're at a morning BNI meeting or on Facebook, the process is still pretty much the same.

On other networks like LinkedIn, you will come across old college buddies, high school friends or co-workers from previous jobs and have the opportunity to connect with them. Based on information entered in a profile, LinkedIn automatically suggests people you may know. This is a great way to continue building your network with those you may not have otherwise remembered to connect with.

Next, if you have staff, have them repeat this exact same process. This is tapping into the networks of your immediate network. This can generate great activity on an ongoing basis as staff and close contacts start advocating your business and start getting involved on your business page.

However you do it, by connecting with people you already know, you are building your prospecting and referral database for the future.

Define Your Social Media Goals

We hope by now you're starting to get our mantra; in order to survive and thrive in this changing world an Agent needs to utilize the *Traditional* marketing and sales concepts that remain the same while incorporating a full-range of *Digital* branding initiatives in order to become a Tra*digital* Agent.

We have taken you through the steps to get started using social media, but just like anything else in life, you will be more successful if you take a time out and develop specific goals and strategies for your social media campaign. The end product is a strong Agency brand that has helped you connect with hundreds if not thousands of potential customers and keeps you close to those clients you already have.

Without taking the time for this critical process it is easy to end up wasting time, money, and resources. We also know getting a social media campaign set up and running smoothly can seem overwhelming. That's why it's important to define what you want to accomplish with social media.

Let's start at the beginning, again. First, the good news! As you can see from the discussion above, social media has a very low barrier to entry.

Now here's the bad news. It is just as easy to invest a lot of time doing the wrong things and achieve *under*whelming results. That's why having clearly defined goals and a strategy is extremely important.

Social media works most effectively when it is one of *many* tools used to market and grow an agency. To be most effective, social media is best used to enhance any marketing strategies and goals already in place. Since social media needs to become part of an existing agency marketing plan, its usage should be aligned with the overall growth and retention strategy for the agency.

No matter what your agency goals are, social media can help meet and exceed them. In the introduction, we gave you a list of five elements of business that we feel social media can help you with. If you look at them again, you will see they are the top five broad goals for any insurance agent:

- Increase Prospecting and Opportunities for Sales
- Increase Customer Service
- Improve Retention and Cross Sales
- Gain Referrals
- Humanize Your Agency Brand

When you start outlining your goals for social media, these are the five elements you want to concentrate on, and by using this list, you can make some specific and results-based goals for yourself. For example, answer the following questions:

- Do you want to grow your Commercial book? By what percent?
- Improve retention? How much? By when?
- Prospect for new clients? How many? In what time period?
- Gain referrals? What type? From whom?

It may be helpful to write your answers down and keep them in mind as we move on to determining your social media strategy.

Define your Social Media Strategy

Once you have the big goals identified with the questions above, you can start creating a strategy for achieving those goals. Always remember, the first step in determining your social media strategy is to determine which platform(s) you will use. Keep in mind, if you are interested in more than one, you don't have to deploy them all at once. In fact, we recommend starting with just one and getting the hang of that platform for two to three months before adding another one.

While we recommend starting with Facebook, whether you start with that or another platform doesn't matter. What does matter is that you deploy your social media platforms in an organized manner so you can keep up with the maintenance of them daily. A Twitter account that you never use to send Tweets is useless and a LinkedIn account won't do you any good if you don't connect with clients or prospects, engage in LinkedIn groups, and utilize the other valuable features of this networking platform.

So the very basis of your social media strategy is that you decide to use it, preferably daily, and in a way that engages your intended audience.

Who Is The Target Audience?

To know how to engage your target audience, you need to define who your target audience actually is. The answer to this question is going to be based on your agency's goals.

Think about your agency's strengths and any specialties catered to. For instance, a P&C agent will likely want to reach out to families, homeowners and drivers. A Health Insurance agent may want to target small business owners and those who work for small businesses that don't offer benefits.

However, don't leave out your first and best target audience. Sometimes called our "natural market" these are family and friends who have similar interests, trust us with their business and will refer us to others (more to follow on how to build a fan base with these contacts in Chapter Six).

Identifying your target audience allows you to tailor, or "niche," your marketing message to the needs of that audience (just like you would do in traditional forms of marketing, right?)

Be sure to consider their likes, dislikes, interests, and concerns. As an example, senior citizens are the fastest growing demographic on Facebook. They like images and stories, and because this demographic stays on your page longer than others, they are likely to read any blogs you refer to, Facebook Notes you write, and they will look at your photo albums. However, they don't like hype or jargon: just the straight, truthful facts for this group.

The twenty-something crowd prefers quick, to-the-point communication. They want a picture or a video that tells them the story, not a lengthy sermon about why they should purchase insurance from you. They don't want you to tell them; they want you to show them, and fast!

The ultimate goal is to eventually end up with a large variety of followers in your social media network, so using just one style of communication won't work. But there is a way around this problem. Simply tailor your message to suit the style of the target audience you're trying to reach at that particular moment in time.

For instance, when posting about life insurance for a young family, keep the message brief as the target audience will be a younger crowd and you won't have their attention for long. If, on the other hand, you want to post a message about Long-Term Care, feel free to make that message a little longer, maybe include a video and a link to your blog post about Long-Term Care. The target audience for this product will likely view all of the information you provide.

Perhaps the most important tip we can give you is one that we already mentioned: be your authentic self. It's funny, but those who frequent social media can easily spot someone who is lazy and posting content just to post it, or worse a phony or a slick salesperson who is more interested in the person's money than helping them buy something of value. Be sure to put your sincere self forward in this public forum and stick with topics in which you have at least a vague interest.

What Do You Hope To Achieve With Each Platform?

Each network offers unique connection opportunities and different ways to interact with clients, prospects and centers of influence. Make sure you understand the benefits and demographics of each platform so you can select the one(s) that best compliments your goals. To help you do that, here is a snapshot of some popular social media platforms explained as it relates to Insurance Agents. Enjoy!

Social Media Explained

 I sell #LifeInsurance

 Here's why you need Life Insurance

 This is where I sell Life Insurance

 My reason for Life Insurance

 Here is a video of me talking about Life Insurance

 My skills include selling Life Insurance

 Here's a picture of a happy family with a touching caption to express how much everyone needs Life Insurance

 This is where I write articles about Life Insurance

 Here's where you request a quote on Life Insurance

 Friendly reminder you need to buy Life Insurance

 Google places This is where people recommend me for Life Insurance

4

Manage Your Social Media for Maximum Results

"Quit counting fans, followers and blog subscribers like bottle caps. Think, instead, about what you're hoping to achieve with and through the community that actually cares about what you're doing."

— Amber Naslund

NOW THAT YOU HAVE THE BASICS DOWN, YOU CAN START thinking about how to manage your social media campaign to keep it from becoming a monster. One of the constant complaints we get in our workshops is that social media is a time suck. It can take over your day, so that is why it is important that your social media strategy includes managing the whole affair so you can obtain maximum results. The following are tips we give our workshop audiences:

Social Media Time Management

None of us have time to sit around and play on the internet all day. We are business owners who have to make money in order to pay our business expenses and make a living. If we were simply playing on social media platforms we wouldn't sell anything, and selling is what keeps our agencies growing.

Don't let social media become a hindrance rather than a help to your agency growth and development. When used strategically with discipline (versus watching funny cat videos, for instance), it can be a great marketing and relationship building tool. This strategic usage is what we are advocating.

At least during work hours, don't get sucked into the time wasting temptation of social media. Refreshing your screen every thirty seconds and then commenting on every new post from friends won't bring in any new business. During business hours it's important to work strategically while spending time on social media networks. Here are some ideas to help you create and stick to a plan:

1. Have specific daily, weekly and monthly social media goals and a self-monitoring mechanism in place. Goals we have seen work include such items as:

   a. Connect with one existing "center of influence" each day.

   b. Write a LinkedIn recommendation for two small business owners each week.

   c. Reach out to one new referral source each day.

Doing these kinds of activities will help you use your social media time strategically.

To help you do this, we recommend an online software called PODS. Developed by an insurance agent, this software lets you create and track a personalized daily checklist of items that you want to accomplish each day. You can easily use PODS to create and track your business goals for social media usage. See Chapter Nine for information on how to register for PODS.

2. Allocate time for each network. On some networks such as Facebook and Twitter you will need to post fresh content each day. On others like LinkedIn you will need to upload a list of your new contacts and clients less often, perhaps weekly. For Facebook and Twitter, it's a good idea to post your content and then check it at least twice per day so you can engage with anyone who has left a comment or asked your business a question. LinkedIn is more of a resource you will use as needed, like to prepare for a client meeting.

   Fortunately, there are tools out there that help you organize your Facebook postings and Tweets so you don't have to be constantly writing and posting. One very successful strategy used by many major internet marketing types is to spend an hour a week writing content for social media, loading it into one of the social media tools (like a site called Hootsuite), and telling that site when to actually post the material. However, these tools should never take the place of engaged connections, and if you find that by using them, you aren't as engaged, then revert to manually making your posts daily and keep the conversations fresh. For more information about these tools, please see Appendix A.

3. If your staff is also going to use social media to tap into their own networks and prospect for business, it is critical that you set social media goals and track accomplishments for them as well. Your license with PODS will allow you to set individual goals as well as track actual sales results for each staff member and see detail and summary reports for your whole team.

4. A word about using staff or hiring a company to manage your social media presence. Consumers are using social media to personally connect with friends and family. First, you will need to monitor your staff to make sure they are using social media to forward the agency's goals. But also know when consumers connect with your agency as a small business, they expect a personal touch from you as well. For best results, the agency owner should take responsibility for developing the agency digital brand and voice, then train and monitor their staff or their social media management company on proper usage of that voice and brand.

5. We see a lot of agencies pass on the responsibility of social media management to low- level staff members. This is not a good idea, and the results show it. The posts are usually unemotional, unengaging, and inconsistent. If you must assign some social media responsibility to a staff member, make it the marketing manager who already understands the agency brand you want to project.

6. If you decide to hire a company to manage your digital brand, be sure that you purchase the largest

package of options they have available. They will need to do more than just post content daily; they'll have to create and manage your agency brand and voice, engage with fans, keep all profiles current and updated, connect with referral sources and lots more. It's probably cost-prohibitive for most agents to hire a company that will create a truly personal touch, and in the end it's not something we recommend. Social media is about connecting personally, but if you hire a company to do it, they're not always going to have the passion or the purpose that you do, and it will be evident to your fans.

"Begin With The End In Mind"

Stephen Covey's famous quote is a good one to consider when starting to develop (or retool) a social media brand. Whatever the agency social media goals, "the end" should always include a vision of connecting with others in a sincere way. Whether you are currently utilizing zero, two, or ten types of social media, it is really important to bring a human connection to posts, tweets, and messages.

It is a common misconception that online friends are not real relationships. It is very easy to quickly identify those who feel this way. When viewing their Facebook page it is a long series of posts broadcasting about what they sell, with no user engagement. None of their fans or friends "share" their status updates. No one comments on the posts. In short, no one cares what they say because the business hasn't done anything to show that they recognize their fans as real human beings on the other side of the screen.

Keeping this in mind, your primary goal for everything you do using social media should be to build a genuine friendship with your connections. It is only when this occurs that the true value of social media will begin to show itself.

If you've been unsure of what to post or have been posting content that isn't getting the results you desire, don't worry. It's never too late to change! Changing this one little thing will dramatically ramp up the amount of interest your pages receive, and that's the secret to successfully using social media.

Commitment and Consistency

To be successful using social media, two things are necessary: commitment and consistency. It takes commitment to add social media to your marketing toolbox. Because this method of marketing is so personal, when someone is not genuine or is impatient in their attempt to make connections online it will show. People will sense the insincerity and it won't be an effective marketing platform.

We all have to make a conscious effort to not be just another broadcaster, begging people to buy something. An alternative is to use engaging pictures, videos, and posts to show fans how we have helped others and what we can do for them.

It's going to take some trial and error while you find your audience and tweak your message until you discover how to best connect with your network in a way that feels natural for you. That's perfectly normal—keep at it!

This is where the consistency comes into play. When we talk about being consistent, we mean that there are steps that have to be taken daily to "work" social media. It is not enough to simply create a Facebook page or Twitter account. It will take some time, say thirty minutes each morning and afternoon, looking for or creating quality content, posting it and then engaging with those who interact with your messages.

Just like any other marketing method, this isn't something that can be started and then dropped and still expect to see any results. It's critical to be online creating and sharing content and engaging with people daily or else nothing will happen.

While all these "do's and don'ts" of social media can seem daunting, we will say this: using social media to market is the most fun we have ever had at work. It allows us to get creative, let our personality shine through, and make new friends. But again we caution you. While it can be entertaining, make sure to use the time you have carved out of your workday for social media to do just that. Work. Keep your goals, strategies and brand in mind while using social media professionally so you can achieve the results you desire!

Engage Your Social Media Followers

> *"I've learned that people will forget what you said, people will forget what you did, but people will never forget how you made them feel."*
>
> —Maya Angelou

WE DON'T KNOW HOW MANY TIMES AN AGENT HAS COME up to us and said something to the effect of "I have my Facebook page set up, but nothing is happening." That's because they're either not posting content at all or the content they are posting isn't getting people interested enough to respond.

One of the most frequent questions we are asked is, "What type of content should I post?" This is something everyone struggles with in the beginning, including us.

Content is king on social media, and successful engagement is about good content. To be successful on social media, you need to get a feel for what content is suitable for posting and creating engagement. We recommend posting a wide variety of content type to remain interesting to a wide base of followers.

The basic idea behind content, whether it is original (like a blog post) or shared content (like an article written by someone else) is to create a response from your followers. Engaging them in dialogue will allow you to build rapport.

Remember to post content that others can relate to; content that generates that "me too" response rather than the dreaded, "so what." Additionally, when posting something onto a social media page, it is very important to respond to comments others make in order to continue the conversation with followers. This is your time to shine, to make or strengthen a connection and build a friendship. Take advantage of it! Don't just start a conversation and "walk out of the room." Moderate and participate in the conversation. The payoff is that you could gain or retain a client who may generate referrals for you both online and offline.

When Facebook first became popular it was primarily used by individuals to answer the question "What are you doing now?" Therefore, users constantly answered that question by posting useless content such as, "I'm bored," or "I'm at the doctor's office," or "I'm gonna drink some tea." Those days are long gone. As Facebook and social media have advanced, so have expectations for content. Posts must be much more interesting in order to gain and hold the attention of our fans and friends. To this point, the status box on Facebook now asks, "What's on your mind?", which prompts users to give a little more thought to their status updates than simply listing out what they happen to be doing right now.

The following table provides some guidelines on not only what kind of content to post but also how often. Take a look at the suggestions and give it a try! Get yourself out there and see what kind of responses you get.

Content— Should always include a Photo or Video	Recommended Frequency
Interesting Status Updates that relate to insurance. Sometimes you could still answer the question "What are you doing now?" such as "Checking In" at your office or at an appointment. But be careful about these types of posts. People don't want to know that you are paying bills (or some other mundane task). If you just had an interesting conversation, if something really amazing happened to you, then share. And don't be afraid to ask questions that can elicit meaningful (and not just yes or no) responses. You want to get a conversation going!	20%
Inspirational Items such as Quotes, Videos or Pictures	10%
Announce new blog posts with a link that takes Followers to the blog on your web site.	15%
Check-Ins	5%
Announce Agency/Team/Company Accomplishments, News or Events	15%

Share Community Events or Local Interest Stories	5%
Insurance articles from 3rd party as a proof source	5%
Ask a technical or general question for a product or service referral	10%
Promote others/write LI Recommendation for professionals, centers of influence and referral sources	15%

When deciding what content to post, remember to mix it up. Varied information is more interesting to read than always highlighting the same type messages. Also make a distinct effort not to be pushy or beg for sales. You want to pull a prospect towards you, not push them away. Be natural and engaging, position yourself as the expert, and prospects will seek you out.

Engaging on the Big Three

We've already taken you through the basics of how to get you set up on the "big three" social media networking sites, and have given you some background about each one. What follows is some more detailed information about each of the big three, some tips on how to use them effectively, and the kinds of tools that are available to help you use the sites better.

How to Engage on Facebook

Facebook has been described as the equivalent of having a party for friends at your house. It is a place to connect and share with others. Facebook usage continues to explode and there's no reason why insurance agents can't tap into that enormous marketing power and potential!

We've already told you there are 1.06 billion total users as of March of 2013. But check out these other Facebook statistics:

- 618 million daily active users
- More than 150 billion friend connections on Facebook at the end of March 2012.
- On average more than 350 million photos uploaded to Facebook daily
- An average of 2.7 billion Likes and Comments generated by Facebook users per day
- World Population…#1 China, #2 India, #3 Facebook, #4 USA, #5 Indonesia, #6 Brazil, #7 Twitter.

Let's all agree to accept the fact that Facebook is where our clients, prospects, and centers of influence are spending a large portion of their free time. And when they "like" our business Facebook page or "friend" our personal Facebook profile, they are inviting us into their living rooms. Isn't that an agent's dream? And if you're thinking, "Well that's what happens with door-to-door sales", you're starting to think like a tradigital agent. On Facebook, not only are we able to get to know our clients better, but it is because they invited us to do so. That's any salesperson's dream.

Business Facebook Page

Because it can get a little confusing, the first aspect we want to address on Facebook content is the difference between a personal profile and a business page.

When deciding how you want to use Facebook, please remember that your agency needs to have a business Facebook page. Don't create a personal profile and try to use it for business. If someone has to send you a "friend" request in order to gain access to your business content, most won't bother. Besides, Facebook is becoming more aggressive in forcing users who are incorrectly using a personal profile as a business page to either convert their personal profile to a business page or risk being deleted.

Because there is a difference between a personal page and a business profile, some people take that as liberty to post all sorts of inappropriate material on their personal page thinking that since their business contacts won't be visiting their personal page, it won't matter. Resist the urge. If you're using Facebook for business, we recommend that you stay professional--on both sides. Your personal page can be used to "humanize you." You can show pictures of your kids, your parents, let people know how you think philosophically. Don't post pictures of you drunkenly holding up Margaritas in a bar on your Mexico vacation. As the saying goes, what happens in Vegas ends up on Facebook. We think you get the idea.

Some people also think, mistakenly, that they're not going to reap as much benefit from a business page. Somehow a business page is not as "personal" as a personal profile, so that defeats the purpose of being on Facebook. We beg to differ. Take a look at excerpts from the article "14 Benefits of a Facebook Business Page Over a Personal Profile" by Jon Loomer, who accurately lists the benefits of having a Facebook business page versus a personal profile:

1. **Facebook Insights: Access to Mounds of Data**

   As a business on a personal Facebook profile, you have no access to Facebook Insights. You are unable to export and digest the thousands of rows and columns of information that can help you understand your customer, what they like and don't like, where they are from and when they are online.

2. **Facebook Tabs and Contests**

   With "Facebook tabs," you can use apps to explain more about who you are. Provide a video introduction. Feature your products. Provide a newsletter opt-in form. Highlight the history of your company. Without this on a personal profile, how exactly do you do this? You're limited only to your posts to tell your story and sell your products.

3. **Facebook Offers**

   A great way to get some viral buzz going about your business is to run "Facebook Offers." It's an official way to promote a deal you have to your Facebook audience. And when your fans and non-fans claim these offers, their friends see it.

4. **Profiles Limited to 5,000 "Friends"**

   Since you are limited to 5,000 "friends," you are seriously limited by your reach. I don't care if you're a small business with only one location. Everyone has plans to grow, and every business should have the potential growth to want to reach more than 5,000 people on Facebook. If you do, you'll need to scale.

5. **Profiles Look Unprofessional**

I know, I know. You think everyone who "friends" your business appreciates that you are running it through a personal profile. But the truth is that many of us look at it and shake our heads.

It looks sloppy. It's bad planning. It screams, *I don't know what I'm doing!* And these are not the messages that you want to be sending to customers and potential customers.

6. **Access to Advertising**

Oh, I know what you're thinking...**I refuse to give Facebook a dollar of my hard-earned money!** This is probably why you're using a personal profile in the first place. You think that you're reaching more people with a profile than you would with your Page. And you believe that your reach as a Page is diminished intentionally to "force" you to buy advertising.

You know, that EdgeRank Bogeyman. The truth is that EdgeRank impacts personal profiles as well as business pages. By default, your "friends" are set to view "most" of your updates (not "all").

Do you think your posts are reaching more than 16 percent of your "friends" with your personal profile?

If you use a Facebook Page, you can reach more of your Fans and you can reach friends of those Fans with Promoted Posts. You can create ads that target people with relevant interests and attract new fans and new customers.

You can do all of this on a very minimal budget. If you're serious about growing your business, reaching new people and selling your products, you should be open to Facebook advertising.

7. **Privacy Considerations**

   Most people set their default privacy to reveal a lot of personal information only to their Friends. So when they become friends with businesses, they are revealing this information to them.

   Maybe you aren't concerned about the privacy of your customers. Maybe you are ticked by the fact that you have no access to this private information as a business Page.

   But my guess is that if you were to poll your customers, they don't want you to have access to this stuff. By using a profile instead of a Page, you're inviting privacy complaints.

8. **Ability to Assign Admin Roles**

   If you use Facebook as a business Page instead of a personal profile, you open the door to assigning admin roles based on the following:

   - *Insights Analyst:* View Insights
   - *Advertiser:* View Insights and create ads
   - *Moderator:* All of the above, plus send messages as the Page and respond to and delete comments
   - *Content Creator:* All of the above, plus create posts as the Page, edit the Page and add apps
   - *Manager:* All of the Above, plus Manage Admin Roles

If you have an employee or multiple employees who you want to help manage the account, you simply assign roles to them. You would make them "Content Creators" or "Moderators" so that if they leave the company on bad terms, they don't destroy your business' reputation in the process.

If you need help with advertising, you can also bring in a consultant and assign them the Advertiser role. Or only allow someone to see statistics as an Insights Analyst.

9. **Native Facebook Scheduling**

   A great tool is the ability to schedule content within Facebook. I'm using it a ton these days, and it makes my life as a marketer so much easier.

   If you are promoting your business as a Facebook profile, you don't have access to native scheduling. Sure, you could use a third party tool, but your posts will always appear with that third party's formatting and icon. It will be clear that it wasn't posted from Facebook.

   It simply looks better when your posts come from Facebook. The difference in engagement may not be huge, but there is a difference.

10. **Connection to Facebook Places**

    When you set up your business properly, you can also connect your Page to a Place. As a result, the days and hours of operation are visible under your Cover Photo. Very helpful stuff for any customer who comes to your Page.

By setting up your business as a Place, customers can also check in, alerting their friends that they are at your store or restaurant. This is a great way to allow your customers to naturally promote your business.

11. **Business Relevant Information**

From my Timeline, I read this morning that it was *[Business X]'s Birthday Today*. Well, that's kinda weird. It's just silly. When you set up a business as a personal profile, your business now has a gender and a birthday. When you set it up as a business Page, it has a category, a mission statement, products, awards and Founded date. No birthday. No gender.

If you want your customer to learn more about your company and what you do, set up a business Page. If you don't, set up a birthday and gender.

12. **Business Relevant Options**

Like I said, there's a long list of benefits to setting your business up as a Page on Facebook. Some of these benefits are small, but they add up quickly.

With a business Page, you can restrict your audience by country and age. You have access to moderation and profanity blacklists to control the conversation.

You set up your business as a personal profile? No access to this stuff.

13. **Use of Third Party Tools**

There are some terrific third party tools out there that help you better manage your business on Facebook. These tools will help you with content management and planning, analytics, contest promotions and advertising. One of my favorite such tools is AgoraPulse.

These tools also assume you set up your business the right way with a Facebook Page. Set up as a personal profile? No such access.

14. **Avoid Being Shut Down**

Let's assume for a moment that you've gotten through numbers 1–13 of this list and are still oblivious. You're standing firm. You, for whatever reason, still don't see the advantage of representing your business with a Facebook Page.

Well, then risk getting shut down. If running your business through your profile is so great, you will lose something of value. Facebook will take it away.

If what you are doing is something worth keeping, you need to convert your profile to a Page. [9]

As you can see, there are many benefits to using a Facebook business page the way it was designed instead of trying to make a personal profile double as a business page.

Facebook Content

There are two basic ways to engage people on Facebook. They are: 1) To create valuable content and then respond to comments that the content generates and 2) To participate in discussions that friend's post.

For starters, when on Facebook please be sure to only post new content once or twice per day. Many Agents find that mornings and afternoons work well for this. On Facebook

[9] Jon Loomer. "14 Benefits of a Facebook Business Page Over a Personal Profile." www.JonLoomer.com. September 3, 2012. http://www.jonloomer.com/2012/09/03/benefits-of-a-facebook-business-page/

it's not the quantity but the quality of the content that is most important. Checking and posting to Facebook can be the first thing you do in the morning and the last thing you do in the afternoon each workday.

While you are online each morning and afternoon, also scan the Facebook "News Feed" for interesting discussions that you can contribute to. Be sure to use the "Like" button to show your support or agreement for statuses, comments, pictures, videos and links that your friends post. And don't forget to add comments to discussions that others are having. Just like you would do offline (in the real world), participate in the discussion and create new ones! Simply reading other people's posts and comments but not participating is the equivalent of going to a birthday party and sitting in the corner all night. Be sure when you are spending time on Facebook that you get out of the corner and SOCIALize.

GM had to learn this the hard way, like by spending $10 million dollars per year. Their lesson: Facebook is not a place to overtly advertise. You may remember seeing the news in May, 2012 that GM announced it was pulling out of its Facebook ad campaign, stating that the ads didn't work. This was a very controversial move, especially because it came the night before Facebook's much anticipated IPO. Here is part of the statement released by GM at that time as found on http://www.forbes.com/sites/joannmuller/2012/05/15/gm-says-facebook-ads-dont-work-pulls-10-million-account/.

In a statement, GM said: "In terms of Facebook specifically, while we currently do not plan to continue with advertising, we remain committed to an aggressive content strategy through all of our products and brands, as it continues to be a very effective tool for engaging with our customers."

Hmmm, did you catch that last part? GM figured out that people who are on Facebook for fun don't want to be blatantly sold to. They do, however, want to be engaged with others. GM even said "it continues to be a very effective tool for engaging with our customers"(emphasis ours). Let's keep reading. Take a look at the comments this article generated online about Facebook ads and hard selling on Facebook directly (emphasis ours):

Marcus Huggins 1 month ago: Who pays attention to Facebook ads? I am on Facebook practically every day and I rarely notice the ads. I certainly have never purchased a product based on Facebook ads.

Joann Muller, Forbes Staff, 1 month ago: I hardly ever notice the ads when I'm using Facebook. I think GM is probably right to stop wasting money on ads that people don't click-thru. I agree social media is just one of many ways a company can get its message out. There's probably a knee-jerk reaction among many advertisers who are panicked about the rapid changes in media consumption. Social media is about ENGAGING people in your brand, not selling them a product. I think GM is beginning to learn this.

Stephen Cox, 1 month ago: I can't remember one Facebook ad. Also, many people are using browser extensions that block ads, including those on Facebook. Better to work on the social side of Facebook. Don't treat it like TV.

Ella Gunson, 1 month ago: From my own experience in running campaigns, Facebook ads back in 2010 were a novelty for the user and thus generated a lot of interest (i.e. clicks). I saw some excellent results. But as the ad platform has matured, the CPC is generally increasing and the "industry average" CTR has dropped off. As more brands/companies/businesses use Facebook ads, so the competitiveness of the platform goes up (along with the CPC), and all the while Facebook users become more disinterested.

Users have become more savvy to online marketing generally, but I would say they're probably tired of pointless/generic ads or ones that often tell the user to "like" this and "like" that. And I think a brand or business that has a Facebook presence based on direct selling will likely not succeed (perhaps as seen in the drying up of Facebook shops). For me, the most effective use is put to raising brand awareness, promoting particular campaigns, as well as providing customer service, etc. And the ads need to reflect that too. Direct selling on Facebook never seems to do well—users don't like their space being invaded by commercial and corporate enterprise. Where is the incentive to interact with a brand unless there is sterling content, opportunity for customer service and/or a competition? The same goes for ads—what is the incentive to click?

These are only comments from four individuals, but social media experts agree that engaging with a potential buyer and not selling directly to them is the way to go on Facebook.

People are on Facebook to have fun and connect with friends and brands that they like and are interested in.

Facebook is a place to sincerely engage with them, not to do a hard sell on them. But that's not to say that sales don't happen on Facebook. It's just that they happen naturally and *not* because of a pushy sales pitch. And never, ever use a personal event, either happy or tragic, as a way to remind someone of the importance of insurance. (We will mention this point in various places because it bears repeating. It is a common mistake insurance agents make on Facebook.)

No matter what you post, always remember to be sincere and positive when engaging with people. Facebook is a very effective way to interact with potential new clients and can help retain a client and keep us in the front of their mind for referrals. If you take the time to really get in communication with your Facebook followers, you will undoubtedly get some business directly on the Facebook platform.

How to Engage on Twitter

Twitter is like a giant global shopping mall where millions of people are speaking and broadcasting at the same time. There are a lot of Twitter naysayers out there who complain that Twitter is a waste of time because of the constant feed you get at such a fast pace. They just don't know how to use it effectively.

Twitter is a great social media platform to use to encounter new prospects and generate fresh leads. There are hundreds of millions of people on Twitter and they are there looking for interesting people and brands to follow. It is full of people who are not a part of any of your existing networks or databases, and you can follow them without needing any type of action or acceptance from them.

Twitter is called a micro blog and it allows you to post content in 140 characters or less. Why use it? A Forrester report revealed that *"Twitterers are the connected of the connected, overindexing at all social media habits. For example, Twitterers are three times more likely to be Creators (people who create and share content via blog posts and YouTube) as the general US population."*[10]

There are certain strategies and tactics that you can use to engage people on Twitter and we will look at them in detail in this section to help explain the method behind the madness of this very eclectic site. Here are some of the stats:

- There are over 500 million accounts
- 177 million tweets are sent daily
- 1 million accounts are added to Twitter every day
- The top 3 countries on Twitter are USA at 107 million, Brazil at 33 million and Japan at nearly 30 million
- 3 years, 2 months and 1 day...the time it took from the first tweet to the billionth tweet. It now takes only 5 days for users to send a billion Tweets.
- Busiest event in Twitter's history is now "Castle in the Sky" TV screening 25,088 tweets per second (previous record was the last minutes of the 2012 Superbowl with 10,245 tweets per second).

Not convinced yet? Here are more stats and tips. "Eight percent of US online adults post and read updates on Twitter at least monthly, while another 4% read but don't post. While modest, both of these groups will prove powerful for marketers to tap. They're influential and highly active

---

[10] Hogshead, Sally. Fascinate: Your 7 Triggers to Persuasion and Captivation. 2010. Print.

in social applications. Moreover, these tweeters want to interact with you: 26% say they recently started to follow a company on Twitter. To tap this channel profitably, concentrate on delivering value, not just promoting your brand. Quickly engage people who mention your brand, share content worth tweeting about, recognize what tweets work, and dedicate staff to managing your Twitter presence."[11]

Twitter is a unique network where there is great potential to meet new contacts and connect with existing ones. However, it is probably most challenging to engage people on Twitter as compared to other networks. One of the reasons is because there is a lot of random activity on Twitter.

A lot of insurance agents who join Twitter fall into the temptation of becoming another broadcaster, and typical tweets can consist of trying to sell insurance products and services. These messages get lost in the noise and never generate any sales or meaningful connections.

However, there are ways to cut through the noise. The first is by learning to manage the massive flow of information that occurs on Twitter. There are several tools and strategies available to make this flow manageable. These tools can help you engage with other tweeps (your Twitter followers: Twitter + Peeps = Tweeps) in a systematic way.

The most effective strategy to manage Twitter is to segment the flow of incoming content by grouping people together in a logical way. This allows you to look at slices of information that flow via Twitter. In other words, instead of looking at the whole stream of all of your tweeps, you look

[11] xiBlog. Sally Hogshead. CEO & Founder of HowtoFascinate.com. "The Worst First Mistake." SallyHogshead.com. June 4, 2012. http://sallyhogshead.com/hogblog/the-worst-first-mistake

at a small section of the stream and that helps in connecting with a limited number of selected people.

As an agent, you may have thousands of followers and you may follow thousands of people. However, there are probably only a few hundred of them that are high quality prospects or referral sources that you want to follow closely. To segment contacts and incoming content, here are a couple of strategies and tools you can use.

The first way to do this is to use the "List" feature within Twitter itself. Twitter Lists are a great way to segment how you want to see incoming information. Here is how Twitter describes their List feature: "A list is a curated group of Twitter users. When you click to view a list, you'll see a stream of Tweets from only the users included in that group." Lists can be used to track certain groups of people such as existing clients, new prospects, realtors, mortgage brokers, etc. People can be added to or removed from your lists at any time.

A list is a curated group of Twitter users. You can create your own lists or subscribe to lists created by others. Viewing a list timeline will show you a stream of Tweets from only the users on that list.

Note: Lists are used for **reading Tweets only**. You cannot send or direct a Tweet to members of a list, for only those list members to see.

To create a list:

1. Go to your Lists page. This can be done via the **gear icon** drop down menu in the top right navigation bar or by going to your profile page and clicking on **Lists**.
2. Click **Create list**.
3. Enter the name of your list, a short description of the list, and select if you want the list to be private (only accessible to you) or public (anyone can subscribe to the list).
4. Click **Save list**

Note: List names cannot exceed 25 characters, nor can they begin with a number.

For more information on creating and using Twitter lists, please visit Twitter help about lists: https://support.twitter.com/articles/76460-how-to-use-twitter-lists.

Another useful method for organizing Twitter content is to use a third party application such as Hootsuite. Hootsuite is a social media management system that is free and allows you to easily view streams of content from up to five social media platforms on one screen. In Hootsuite, your data streams can be divided into separate columns based on the lists you already created in Twitter.

Another advantage to using this tool is that you can also post content directly from Hootsuite. So for instance, when you want to post updates on multiple networks like Facebook, Twitter and LinkedIn, it can be done simultaneously from one place within a program like Hootsuite. (See Appendix A for more information on Hootsuite).

Now let's take a look at some methods of engagement to use on Twitter.

Follow Back—On Twitter it is a common courtesy to follow people who start following you. It's a good opportunity to say hi, thank them for the follow, and see if there is a potential to start a conversation. Unless you are a celebrity like Oprah or the President of the United States, people will not continue to follow you if you don't follow them back. This can work against you if you are trying to grow your network. Also, when you have two thousand followers, Twitter only lets you follow 1.2 times the number of followers you have. To be able to continue to grow your followers, it is in your best interest to un-follow people who are not following you back so that you can continue to follow and connect with new people.

Retweet—Reposting someone else's tweet. It is like forwarding an email you find interesting or valuable to your friends. It generates gratitude and opens an opportunity for dialogue. Also, be sure to thank people when they retweet your content.

#FF—Every Friday it is a tradition at Twitter to introduce your best contacts to your followers on Twitter. Be sure to thank people for #FF mentions. People appreciate this and a bond is created over time when it is done consistently. Use this to promote your top ten to fifteen contacts. Using more than that can dilute the effect and take away from the significance of the contacts you promote.

Public Lists—Create public lists in Twitter and add important Contacts to it. It is like giving someone a compliment because now they know you will be following their content more closely and connecting with them more regularly than other people you may follow. Most people appreciate it and are honored to be part of your public lists. Don't put everyone on a list, just the contacts that you want to follow closely. Here's a sample of Angela's lists:

Lists Subscribed to / Member of   Create list

All About Real Estate by Angela Johnson
My list of real estate pros nationwide
47 members

Leading In Lending by Angela Johnson
6 members

Mes Amis by Angela Johnson
9 members

Insurance Tweeps by Angela Johnson
74 members

All Things OWN by Angela Johnson
Everyone I follow related to Oprah and OWN
42 members

Inspirational Ppl by Angela Johnson
13 members

News & Community Services by Angela Johnson
30 members

Fab Food! by Angela Johnson
40 members

#Hashtags—A hashtag can be used to create topic specific discussions. They are specific words that are preceded by the # symbol. Think of them as a TV channel about, for example #autoinsurance or other business related topics. People who are interested in a certain topic can follow the hashtag and are more likely to participate in your conversation.

Caution: don't overuse hashtags. Hashtags are ideal for promoting brands or certain conversations but should not be used to describe what you are doing, such as #iwantadonutrightnow.

That's Twitter in a nutshell. Just remember, the brands that use Twitter effectively are those that tweet useful information. Just like any other platform, to use it effectively be sure to engage in all sides of the communication cycle: sometimes you're sending original information, sometimes you're responding to information, and sometimes you're forwarding information on.

What we have found to be the most useful thing about Twitter is that it is the perfect platform to direct Twitter followers to your Facebook page. Twitter is a good place to make an introduction. Facebook gets them more interested in you and the value you could offer them as a client, and then it becomes a natural step to take the person offline, talk to them directly, and turn them into a client. All this can occur by starting from quick bites of information that are no more than 140 characters long.

We have come to think of Twitter as a little like a tiramisu which means "little pick me up," in Italian. It's a fun break from the more serious task of doing the hard core networking. That job is best left to LinkedIn.

How to Engage on LinkedIn

As an Insurance Professional, LinkedIn is an essential part of building your digital brand. LinkedIn describes itself as the "World's largest professional network". If Facebook is like having a party at your house and Twitter is like shopping at a global mall, then LinkedIn is like attending a giant Chamber of Commerce meeting. LinkedIn is where traditional networking takes place, online, and it works so much like traditional networking, it's amazing.

Let's look at some LinkedIn facts from their web site:

Company Background

- LinkedIn started out in the living room of co-founder Reid Hoffman in 2002.

- The site officially launched on May 5, 2003. At the end of the first month in operation, LinkedIn had a total of 4,500 members in the network.

- As of December 19, 2012 (the end of the first quarter), professionals are signing up to join LinkedIn at a rate of approximately two new members per second.

LinkedIn Facts

- As of December 19, 2012, LinkedIn operates the world's largest professional network on the Internet with 187 million members in over 200 countries and territories.

- USA leads membership at more than 72 million, Europe has more than 34 million members

- LinkedIn members did nearly 4.2 billion professionally-oriented searches on the platform in 2011 and were on pace to surpass 5.3 billion in 2012.

LinkedIn and Business

- LinkedIn counts executives from all 2011 Fortune 500 companies as members; its corporate hiring solutions are used by 82 of the Fortune 100 companies.
- LinkedIn represents a valuable demographic for marketers with an affluent & influential membership.
- As of March 31, 2012, there are more than 1.3 million unique domains actively using the LinkedIn Share button on their sites to send content into the LinkedIn platform.
- LinkedIn members are sharing insights and knowledge in more than one million LinkedIn Groups.

WHEW! That's a lot of information. But we gave it to you to underscore the importance of you developing a LinkedIn presence. It is serious networking but it can also be fun; especially if "fun" for you is closing new business, finding new prospects or hiring qualified, professional team members!

Let's recap: LinkedIn is an excellent place to connect with professionals. Most insurance agents we know need and want most or all of their business to come from clients who understand and appreciate the need for insurance and can afford to pay for it. That sounds exactly like the type of people who are on LinkedIn.

Get the Most out of LinkedIn

Profile—While we've already covered this topic in Chapter Three, we want to touch on it again here because your profile on LinkedIn is the make-break point. Thoroughly complete your entire LinkedIn Profile. The more information you enter on your profile, the more connections LinkedIn can recommend for you. Remember to include a picture, description, education, current & past positions, web site, summary, skills & expertise, honors & awards and contact information. A completed profile will also help others find you. We can't stress enough how important it is that you don't leave your profile unfinished. That would be the equivalent of mailing out an incomplete resume or telling potential candidates about only part of your expertise.

Your LinkedIn connections want to get an idea of the kind of professional you are when they view your profile. Allowing them to scan your profile accomplishes this easily. If it is only partially completed, this could send the message that you aren't thorough or don't follow through on tasks. Of all the social media platforms, Linked In is the place to put your most professional profile forward so prospects and clients can get a full picture of your Agency, beyond what they are able to see on Facebook or Twitter.

Recommendations—LinkedIn is an excellent place to network with "affluent and influential" people as well as do some B2B prospecting. As with any social media platform, you only get out of it what you put into it. This is particularly important for the feature of LinkedIn called recommendations. These are testimonials that others write about you and your agency. We have found that the best way to gently nudge people to write a recommendation for you is to first write recommendations for others.

A few LinkedIn recommendations can be a powerful tool when someone is doing research on your agency before deciding whether or not to do business with you. You can also use your recommendations in a sales presentation. For instance, simply print your recommendations and show them to a client who asks what he/she can expect if they choose you as their agent. These testimonials to your professionalism and customer service can be just what is needed to move someone off the fence into a buying decision.

(client)
Sharon hired you as a Insurance Agent in 2010

Top qualities: **Personable, Expert, High Integrity**
"Thru Angela's expertise in the Insurance business, I felt I was in good hands. She was very detailed in explaining my policy and all my concerns. I highly recommend her for all your insurance needs. Sharon " *July 5, 2012*

Cross-Pollinating—Another way to grow your LinkedIn connections is to invite others to connect with you. This can be done by posting a link to your LinkedIn profile on your other social media networks such as Facebook and Twitter. To do this, go to your LinkedIn profile. In the top part to the right of your picture, there are two buttons that say Improve Your Profile and Edit. Click on Edit and then Share Profile. Then select Facebook and/or Twitter to post a link to your LinkedIn profile to those networks.

Share

Check out my professional profile and connect with me on LinkedIn.
http://lnkd.in/E3V9fU

f Share   ✓ Tweet   Close

Groups—LinkedIn has a great feature called Groups. Because LinkedIn is designed as a networking tool, joining and contributing to the group conversations in groups is important. There are groups for almost anything you can imagine, from local small business owners to sororities. When you join groups that you are qualified to be part of and contribute to the discussions, people will begin to seek you out to help them with their insurance needs.

Insurance Plan Reviews—As insurance professionals, we all like to conduct periodic reviews with our clients. LinkedIn helps make these reviews more personal and productive.

Imagine you are prospecting for life insurance. Because of the information available on LinkedIn, you can easily see that a client has changed jobs, which may prompt a need for insurance changes. You know this because of their LinkedIn profile and can easily lead into a discussion of appropriate products.

Another useful example is when preparing to meet with a business owner for your insurance presentation, you can ask more meaningful questions based on all the basic information about their business that you have collected from their LinkedIn profile. This step puts you far ahead in your client's mind as an interested party and trusted advisor vs. someone who walks into their office and hasn't done their homework.

Communication is the Key

There is so much that you can do on these networking sites in terms of content—too much to put in a book that's designed to get you up and running. It's one of the reasons we created a subscription site, http://www.goingtradigital.com/ to give you step by step how-to videos on using social media to grow your agency bigger and stronger.

For now, what we really want you to do is just get started! If you haven't yet created a social media presence, we invite you to do so now. Once you have your business Facebook page created or your LinkedIn profile up, start posting! If you make a mistake, don't worry about it. Like we said earlier, we've made all the mistakes in the book, and we're still alive, still in business and able to talk about it. Sometimes, you just have to dive in, and social media is definitely that kind of a deal.

You probably have an idea of what's going to work best for you based on your personality and ideal client profile. Each platform has specific functions they are better at than others, and it takes some commitment to make each platform work for you.

Don't let yourself get overwhelmed. Again, start with one platform, get used to it, and then start creating your profile and presence on the next one. And remember, at the heart of it all is communication. Good communication breeds good connections. Be interested first so that others find you interesting. To be interested, remember to engage with your contacts, initiating, participating in and moderating discussions. To be interesting you need to post varied content that is informative.

Building your digital brand is entirely possible with social media. If you feel like it's still overwhelming, go back, review this chapter, and then post something on one or all of your social media channels. Don't be discouraged if you don't get immediate feedback. It may take a week or two of consistent, daily posts for people to trust that if they comment on your content you will respond in a way that is interesting to them.

It will take some practice to develop your online voice and brand. That's okay, we've all been there and we're all constantly growing and getting better at this interactive form of online communication marketing.

Oh, and one more thing. If after reading this chapter you are now feeling like you are part of the large group of businesses who have not been making the most of their social media usage, please don't be disheartened. Today is the first day of the rest of your social media life, and it is going to take some practice to get it just right. Play around with it, have fun and BE SOCIAL.

Increase Prospecting and Opportunities for Sales

"You don't close a sale, you open a relationship if you want to build a long-term, successful enterprise."

—Patricia Frip

You've got your social media pages set up. You have invited all of your friends and clients. You've posted some engaging content. Now what? Well, what's the very first item on any salesperson's agenda? Finding new prospects.

The tricky, grueling and yet exciting thing about a career in sales is that every time you gain one new client, you lose one prospect. The ongoing need to feed the prospect beast can be challenging for insurance agents, but is critical to our ongoing success.

Think about all the ways you have traditionally worked to feed the prospect beast. You go to those ridiculously early networking meetings or sit through countless (and too often boring) chamber of commerce meetings. You might do direct mail or phone surveys. You constantly talk about anything and everything having to do with insurance to anyone who cares to listen. To be successful, you have to be on constant alert for new prospecting opportunities.

The goal of networking, direct mail, or any other prospecting mechanism we could think up has always been to generate new leads. We hope that by now you're already starting to see how social media can do that as well as any other networking activity. In fact, it can accomplish pretty much the same results of any of the above lists and you can do it from the comfort of your office and it's the price we all like—free (except of course for the value of your time)! But there is one key difference about social media prospecting. We have found that leads resulting from social media platforms are initiated *by the consumer*. Cold calling could never boast that!

Here's how it works. When someone joins your social media networks, this person has already consciously or subconsciously made the decision to do business with you now or in the future. They've done their work; now it's time to do yours. You post interesting, thoughtful content. You comment on other's posts. Over time through interaction and engagement, trust is established, need is reinforced and price becomes less of a consideration with these potential clients.

In one Facebook post, Nadeem posted a YouTube video about life insurance. A Facebook fan that saw the post, contacted Nadeem, and made an appointment for the very next morning. In salesese, that is now a "hot prospect". And hot it was. That appointment resulted in seven permanent life insurance policies, generating over $10K in commission! This doesn't happen every day, but it *does* happen. When a prospect is ready to purchase but is unsure who to call, a status update from you can spur them to action and land them squarely in your lap.

Unfortunately too many agents hear about friends and other agents who are having success with prospects and sales using social media. Looking to duplicate that success, they set up a profile. After importing all their connections and adding their existing friends and clients on their social media networks, they wait patiently for the magic to happen. They wait for leads and quote requests to start pouring in. They're not posting content or worse they are posting boring or insincere content. They are hoping they can generate a large percentage of new business via social media but get upset when it doesn't happen immediately.

Here's a perfect example of what can happen with good content versus bad. The week after one of our social media conferences for insurance agents, an agent friend who Angela has known for years (we'll call her "Nancy") emailed Angela trying to get a grasp on how to incorporate tra*digital* marketing into her agency.

Her email said, "I have a question. It seems that maintaining a social presence takes a lot of time. Do you pay someone to tweet and post? Or do you do it all yourself? What is the best approach?"

Nancy started a business Facebook page over two years ago with no results. Because she wasn't getting any engagement from fans or selling any new business from her Facebook page, she was having trouble figuring out how and why to use social media as a marketing source.

Angela had seen her business Facebook page in the past and knew that she was using canned, pre-written, generic content. She specifically recalled one post about the opening night of the TV show *Duck Dynasty*. While it's sometimes fun to get in on a pop culture conversation, that wasn't a show Nancy was likely to watch, at all. And those who were following her Page knew it.

Angela reminded her that social media users have a very high sensitivity to knowing what is genuine and what is not. Because Nancy wasn't taking the time to post content that shows the passion she has for her business, her community and clients, her Facebook fans unconsciously decided they wouldn't go out of their way to respond and engage with what she had been posting.

Nancy told Angela months prior that her agency was celebrating a milestone anniversary. Angela reminded her that was great information to share on Facebook.

That afternoon Nancy emailed Angela and was very excited. She said she really took the message to heart and had spent some time working on her Facebook page. When Angela went to Nancy's page, she was thrilled to see that Nancy had created a profile picture highlighting the agency's anniversary. Nancy had also posted a picture of her family and a message that said she was honored to be continuing a family tradition. The response the agent got on that post was incredible. It had more engagement than most anything on her page ever had.

Now the point we're making isn't to exploit relatives who have passed away for more user engagement. The takeaway here is that when you speak to your fans from the heart they will respond. Like any other form of marketing and networking, you get out of social media what you put into it.

Direct Mail/Direct Contact

To give you an example of what we're talking about in terms of the effectiveness of using social media for prospecting, let's look at a very successful traditional prospecting technique and how you could easily take it online: the direct mail campaign. Angela grew her agency by doing direct mail marketing. She got good results from this program for many years and was one of the fastest, steadiest growing agents in South Texas. However, she also realized that direct mail can get very expensive very fast.

Sometimes it can be shocking to stop and calculate the acquisition cost of a new insurance client. Angela knew how much she spent per month on all of the costs associated with the mailings. There was the cost of the bulk mail permit, the lease for the folding machine and copier, the labor to run the folding machine and take the letters to the post office, the cost of paper, postage, and envelopes. But as the years went on and she had gathered all of the low hanging fruit, a wise friend suggested she calculate the current cost of acquiring a new client. Can you believe it was $167?

Now, Angela still does direct mailing. She's a P&C agent, and mailing directly to her community does generate leads. However, she's also taken the idea behind her direct mailer and has posted the same information online. It works well because the centerpiece of both the mailer and online information is the story of her grandparents and how the trademark of their agency was customer service. She even has a great set of pictures of her grandparents to personalize the piece even more. When she posts the information from the mailer online it gets results. When she sends out the mailer it still gets results. The latter costs money, the former costs time—but that's what we have to spend to ensure our agencies have a constantly filled prospect pipeline. And that's what makes Angela a successful tra*digital* agent!

Mistakes in Prospecting: Proceed with Caution

We have said it before and we'll probably say it again. We have made lots of missteps when it comes to social media posts. It is our hope that by providing our readers with these humiliating failures we can shorten your learning curve and save you from the same embarrassment. Here are some of the biggies in prospecting:

Death by Broadcasting

Creating a profile and adding contacts to social media networks is like creating a form letter but not putting anything personal into it. The key is to engage potential prospects in sincere, meaningful exchanges. What do we mean by that? Think of it this way. There are two types of communication. The first, and undesirable, is what we call broadcasting. This is one major mistake that many people make when they're posting online content we hope that you avoid doing. "Broadcasting."

When someone broadcasts, they are not having a conversation *with* you, they are talking *at* you. It is simply a full-on sales pitch that is constantly streaming out on your posts with no personalization attached to it. While it may work for commercials, it is the kiss of death in the social media community. Here's why.

Have you ever been trapped by someone who never stopped talking, not even to take a breath? They don't ask a single question about you, your likes, dislikes, family, career. Nothing. They just drone on and on about themselves. If you're like most, you find these people to be *boring*. When trapped by these people at a party or event you look desperately around the room for someone to save you. It can feel like hours, and finally some poor unknowing soul walks up and you make your escape, feeling kind of guilty for leaving them there all alone with the "broadcaster," but you're not willing to go back and rescue them.

As sales people, it is very tempting to use social media to start broadcasting sales messages such as, "Call me for a free auto quote!" or "Looking for the best insurance agent in Texas? Call me!" It's only natural to think that if we have an audience and we want to sell them something, the most logical thing to do is to ask them to call us, right? We've tried that and all we can say is: Resist the urge! After all, aren't all insurance quotes free? And doesn't everyone think they are the best insurance agent in (fill in the blank). Because there is no *compelling* call to action in these type broadcasts, your message will be ignored.

We think you get the idea of what happens when you have someone who is droning on and on about how great their product is and how everyone should buy it.

Engage

The second, most desirable type of communication is engaging. When posts on social media are engaging, it is when you're interested in the people you're reaching out to instead of trying really hard to be interesting. When someone is engaging you in conversation there is give and take, questions and answers, thoughtful consideration, listening and responding. *That* is what we must do when using social media. Think of it as a conversation at a cocktail party. No one wants to listen to a broadcaster who is working very hard at being interesting. They want to be engaged in an interesting two-way conversation with someone who is interested in them.

Using Tragedy or Triumphs to Sell Insurance

We want to share the most embarrassing, deep, dark secret Angela has about posting the wrong content on social media. If you promise you can read it and still respect her, read on. This is what happened:

"A friend of mine on Facebook drove past a bad motorcycle wreck and wrote about it on Facebook. He said it appeared that two people were very badly injured, lots of passers-by had stopped to help and there was already an ambulance on the scene so he didn't stop for fear of getting in the way. He then asked everyone to take a minute and say a prayer for the injured people. Several people commented with sweet thoughts and prayers, and I thought it would be a good time to remind people about the importance of life insurance because after all, you never know when an accident can happen. Let me assure you, it was *not* a good time to remind people about the value of life insurance! Although I was only thinking of this post from a business perspective, there were actual people who were injured at that very moment, and that is what everyone was worried about. Not life insurance. And they let me know it."

Angela was very ashamed of herself. She, like you, was trained to listen for life events and key phrases and then use that information as a pivot to a sale. That training can be very difficult to turn off, but there are times when it is not appropriate to pivot to a sale. If the example above had been a live conversation, Angela certainly would not have jumped to a pitch for life insurance. She would have been better able to "feel" that wasn't an appropriate time. It's a little more difficult to "feel" that in an online conversation, so just remember not to be a broadcaster and you'll be fine.

There is a flip side to this, however. If one of your clients has a baby, definitely post a huge "Congratulations" on their wall and then send them a card and maybe even splurge on a gift card of a small bouquet of flowers for them. But do *not* use that as a time to talk about life insurance for the infant. Show that you genuinely care about them. The same holds true if you discover that one of your clients has lost a parent or a loved one. Sending a sympathy card will be something they remember, and you can also post your condolences online or in a private message as well.

When using social media, we all have to keep in mind that this is a real form of communication with real people on the other end receiving our messages. That can be highly advantageous if we use it right and it can be disastrous if we appear as a callous and uncaring opportunist.

Learn to Fascinate

Now, what if you were in a conversation with someone and they asked you a question but then just walked away before you could answer? That would be considered rude, wouldn't it? The same is true on social media channels. When we post content and people begin commenting on it, we have to take advantage of the opportunity for engagement and continue to moderate and contribute to the conversation just as we would do in real life. Does that make sense?

In the insurance field, the end result we are all looking for is to retain existing clients and find new prospects. The question is, what are the steps between making online connections and gaining loyalty and sales? In her bestselling book *Fascinate*, Sally Hogshead talks about the power of full engagement. When a contact, client or center of influence is fully engaged, the results can be outstanding. She says, "Fascinating messages like fascinating people, have the potential to consume us as almost nothing else can, sucking us into a vortex of intensity."[x]

In her June 4, 2012 blog, "The Worst First Mistake," Sally goes on to say, "You've heard that 'time is money.' But I'll take it a step further. *Attention is money*. If you're asking for someone's attention, but fail to deliver value in return, you've just wasted their most precious non-renewable resource."[xi]

Wow! We don't want to waste someone's "most precious non-renewable resource," and we sure don't want ours wasted either. Do you? So how do you avoid that and instead fascinate or engage your audience?

What sets fascinating social media users apart from the broadcasters is exactly the same thing that sets an interested person apart from the person who is trying to be interesting: someone who can listen and engage by communicating something interesting back to the listener. It's the art of good communication. Think about it. Communication 101 says that to be *interesting* you must first be *interested*. The rule of social media 101 is the same. Social media is most effective when it is a give and take relationship developed with online contacts. When you engage in sincere meaningful exchanges, your prospecting ratio goes way up. It's the ideal scene for a sales person: engaging a contact in a meaningful, personalized way starts the process of turning a mere contact into a prospect, a prospect into a client or a client into a referral source.

Please understand that it is more important to have depth than breadth in social media connections. That is, creating real depth with connections is more important than having thousands of connections who never interact with your content.

This is an important mental shift in order to be results-oriented. Someone may not have thousands of contacts on their network, but if they manage to engage with even a few hundred carefully collected contacts the resulting opportunities can be priceless.

When we talk about engagement, we are talking about the emotionally intelligent side of social media. For some agents, it comes naturally and they start connecting online with ease. Others wonder how to get started and are never able to get to the level where they are consistently engaging their contacts.

Bestselling author Dondi Scumaci put it best when she said that as agents become more and more hi-tech, it becomes more important than ever before to learn how to remain hi-touch.[12] One of the essentials of building rapport is explained by renowned author and business philosopher, Jim Rohn. He says that when we communicate to build rapport, the listener should say "me too" versus "so what." In other words, the goal is to find common grounds with our contacts.[13]

Our goal here is to help you get a fast start into using social media productively by learning from our mistakes. Social media users want to engage with successful brands that are generating strong content, not preaching to them about what products they should purchase.

Growing Your Facebook Fans

Before we end this chapter on prospecting, we want to give you some helpful tips on how to use Facebook for that purpose. We've already mentioned that a Facebook page is the place where people will follow you if they are inclined to do business with you in the future, or if they find your content helpful, or they look to you as a trusted insurance professional.

One of the best ways to prospect online is finding ways to increase your fan base on Facebook. In its simplest sense,

---

[12] Scumaci, Dondi. Author of Career Moves, 2010. Print. and Designed for Success, 2008. Print

[13] Jim Rohn, Take Charge of Your Life, The Winner's Seminar, Tape 5, Bridging the Communication Gap, Nightingale-Conant Corporation.

this is a form of opt-in marketing. Opt-in is a standard technique in the internet world. When you sign up on a site to buy something, for example, the site will generate an "opt in" button that you have to click on or select that allows the company to continue to contact you. When people "like" your page, they are indirectly giving you permission to entice them to do business with you. However, this should not be taken as permission to bombard them with a full-fire sales pitch. Not everyone loves insurance as much as we agents do, and the general public definitely doesn't like to be "sold," they would rather "buy."

The simplest way to get your fan base growing is to upload your existing contacts into your Facebook or LinkedIn account as discussed in Chapter Three. There are a few other techniques you can utilize to get the contacts from your personal Facebook profile to become a fan of your business page.

For instance, you can occasionally post the link to your business page onto the wall of your personal profile. This is a gentle reminder to your friends who may have missed the invite to like your business page.

Nadeem Damani

If you haven't already done so, please take a second to go to my biz FB page and click on 'Like button' so we are connected there as well. :)

Damani Insurance Agency

7 Times Championship Award Winner (Awarded to top 3% of Farmers Insurance Agents in the Nation), 10 Times Topper Club Award recipient. Million Dollar Round Table (qualifying member in 2006). www.mdrt.org. I care about my clients and I deliver on my promises. My company, Farmers may not be the least...

Page: 1,275 like this

Like · Comment · Share · about a minute ago · 🌐

You can also use the "Share" feature on posts from your business page to your personal profile that you think your friends may enjoy or find useful. When they click on the post to read it, they are on our business page and will ideally "Like" the page while they are there.

Also, when you post a picture on your business page, make sure to tag yourself in it so that the picture also appears on your personal profile. Your friends then get a notification that you were tagged in a picture. If they view the picture on your business page and they haven't liked your page yet, it's a good reminder to do it while they are already there.

Increase Prospecting and Opportunities for Sales

These are a few ways you can get your friends and family to become fans of your business page and start growing your potential list of prospects. Just as important is the ability to drive those you don't already know to your business page. Facebook allows you to go to the next level by creating an ad for your business page. We discussed ads briefly when we talked about GM's failed social media campaign. You do have to be careful about ads since they cost money, and you should not rely on them exclusively. You can control how much you want to spend. Facebook has a very clear FAQ section so read up before you start placing ads so you're not hit with an unexpected bill. But we have seen them work if they are done in conjunction with good content on your Facebook business page.

To create an ad, go to your business page. Please note that Facebook is always changing so these exact directions are subject to change. However, because this is one way Facebook makes money they probably aren't going to take away the capability to create an ad. If you can't find how to create an ad, check the Facebook Help pages for the latest update!

As of the writing of this book this is how you place an ad; Click on "Build Audience" and then "Create an Ad."

Here's a tip that we have found to be very useful. Once into the ad building section, select the option you prefer but be sure to include Sponsored Stories. This means that an ad for your business page will show up in your friends' News Feeds—and there is the key to successful ads on Facebook. If your friends "like" your ad, they'll click back to your page or interact with a post. The ad needs to be interesting, funny, thought provoking, something to get people to "like" it and send it on to their friends. Think of this as a referral. It is like your friend is saying, "I like this person and you should too."

Continuing on through the Ad-building process, you can select who you want the ad to go to by lots of factors, like city, interests, age or a combination of all three.

Once you have selected your target audience, move on to naming your campaign. This will help once you have more created and run more than one ad. By naming the ad campaigns, you can easily tell each ad apart when viewing them on the results page in Facebook so you will be able to tell which ads are effective and which ones aren't.

Set your campaign budget, campaign schedule and then either Review the ad or Place your order. The staff at Facebook will review your ad to make sure it complies with their guidelines and then approve it. Your ad won't begin running until approved. The approval process normally takes just a few hours.

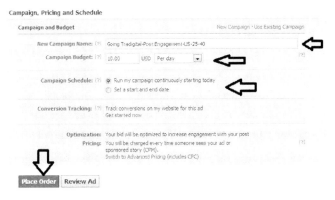

This is how word spreads on social media networks. Friends tell friends about a good company, brand or web site and then those friends tell their friends, and so on. The next thing you know, you have people liking your business Page on Facebook, following you on Twitter, and paying attention to you on LinkedIn. You have prospects that you can cultivate a relationship with and eventually lead them down the sales funnel to a close until you have created a new client.

Prospecting On Twitter

A great way to search for new prospects on Twitter is to use the Search feature within Twitter for key words or phrases. Take some time to write down popular keyword searches of products you offer and think your clients or prospects may tweet about.

Once you have a few items on your list, try them one at a time in the Twitter search bar, see below.

In this instance, the search phrase "moving to Texas" returned many tweets from people who are moving to Texas in the near future. To begin a dialogue with this future client (gotta remain confident, right?), I sent him a tweet welcoming him to Texas and offered a link to a blog I wrote about Texas homeowners insurance.

Remember, on social media, as in real life, it's more effective to become a resource to someone than it is to immediately ask for a sale. Those who just use Twitter to broadcast won't succeed in closing sales. It's important to pull people toward you rather than turn them off with a sales pitch and push them away.

Searching for Prospects on LinkedIn

There are many ways to utilize LinkedIn for new client prospecting. Let's go over a few of them.

Just as searches are a good way to prospect on Twitter, they are also a great prospecting tool on LinkedIn. As you can see below, a search can be performed based on many basic categories. For instance, you can search for LinkedIn members within your zip code and then send them InMail (the email system within LinkedIn) to introduce yourself, provide useful content or ask for the opportunity to earn their business.

In order to be able to be able to contact anyone using InMail, you'll have to sign up for a paid subscription to LinkedIn. However, this small subscription charge is worth it because statistics

show that InMail is thirty times more likely to receive a response than a cold call.

There are also additional items available with the Advanced Search feature. Suppose you want to locate CPA's in your area and begin connecting with them. The Advanced People Search in LinkedIn provides many choices that will narrow down your search to help you make the right connections.

Advanced People Search

Relationship

- ✔ 1st Connections
- ✔ 2nd Connections
- ✔ Group Members
- ☐ 3rd + Everyone Else

Location

Current Company

Industry

- ☐ Accounting
- ☐ Airlines/Aviation
- ☐ Alternative Dispute Resolution
- ☐ Alternative Medicine
- ☐ Animation

Past Company

School

Profile Language

- ☐ English
- ☐ Spanish
- ☐ German
- ☐ French
- ☐ Italian

Let's talk about some tips LinkedIn suggests to keep in mind when writing InMails.

- Your InMail should be a conversation starter. Don't expect to or try to close the deal during the first contact.

- Be conversational and enthusiastic, seeking to elicit that "me too" response rather than "so what".

- Be brief and concise.

- Give them a reason to reply. By ending your InMail with a question you will increase the likelihood of starting a conversation.

LinkedIn Introductions

If you would like to connect with and get to know someone who you aren't connected to (and don't already know), you can do two things. Join a group they are part of or ask another member who is connected to that person to make an introduction. This is as close to real world networking as you can get! Just as an introduction is powerful at a Chamber of Commerce meeting, so they are on LinkedIn.

Here are the steps to follow in order to request an introduction:

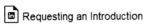 Requesting an Introduction

How do I request an introduction to someone I'm not currently connected to?

Last Reviewed: 08/21/2012 · Report Answer Inaccuracies

An introduction lets you contact members who are in your 2nd degree network or 3rd degree network. If a member is within your extended network, you can contact them through connections you have in common.

1. Locate the member's profile.
2. Click "Get introduced through a connection" on the right side of the profile.
3. If only one person can make the introduction, the **Request an Introduction** page will appear.
4. Move your cursor over the arrow next to the **Send InMail** button and click **Get introduced**
5. If more than one person can make the introduction, you may choose who you want to make the introduction.
6. Enter a subject for your message.
7. Write a message to the person who will introduce you and be clear about why you're asking for an introduction. This message may eventually be seen by the person you want to be introduced to.
8. Click **Send Request**

If the member isn't within your network, you might be able to click the Send InMail link to contact them. Also, if the member is in a shared group with you, you can send a message to them directly.

By requesting introductions to key people, you can increase your base of prospects and begin working them down your sales funnel.

Once your prospect has become a client, it's important to make sure they're well taken care of, and that's where we turn to next. Using social media as a channel to provide customer service.

Increase Customer Service

"Our head of social media is the customer."

—McDonald's

WE'VE TALKED ABOUT CREATING NEW BUSINESS PROSPECTS through social media. Now how do we use social media to service and retain existing business? That's what this chapter is all about so let's get started.

As service levels in other industries rise as a result of social media and other digital technologies, we as elite insurance agents also need to look into ways of increasing our service levels. There are tons of ways customer service can be handled thru traditional methods. But customer service now goes way beyond just calling your clients once a year for an insurance review. More and more companies are using social media to identify customer service issues and resolving them on social media platforms. Connecting with clients through social media puts your agency in a position to do just that.

Rising customer expectations are causing many of us to rethink the service we deliver and the value we are able to add for a client. Good customer service can mean the difference between a client renewing her policy and referring his friend or not. Also, in an industry where a few large carriers dominate a big portion of the market and those carriers rely on thousands of agents to deliver the exact same products; customer service may be one of the few distinguishing features that separate us from our peers representing the same company right down the street.

What separates you from the other agents in your area? Take a few minutes to think about it and list out a few. These would be good items to post about on your social media networks. Just do it in a professional manner and speak positively about your agency without any negative talk about other agencies.

What makes social media unique is that it provides us the opportunity to listen and respond to clients and prospects in a way no other form of media has ever done. This has created even more opportunities for businesses to provide WOW customer service. People will pay more for good service. What's more, they'll let others know when they've had a WOW experience on their own personal social media pages, and that kind of direct referral is gold. Superior products and service is why restaurants like Morton's Steakhouse are in business. Otherwise, everyone would just go to Steak-N-Ale, right?

We used Morton's Steakhouse on purpose because it holds center stage in what has become known as The Greatest Customer Service Story Ever Told, by Peter Shankman (the guy who created "HARO" which stands for "help a reporter out," a site for editors and such seeking stories for the newspapers, journals, etc.). The following has been taken from Peter Shankman's blog.[14]

The Greatest Customer Service Story Ever Told, Starring Morton's Steakhouse

The following story is entirely true. More importantly, I swear on my entire professional reputation and all I hold dear to me that the story below was in no way staged, planned in advance, or in any way faked. This is real. And most importantly: This is AMAZING.

When my alarm clock went off at 3:30 this morning, I knew I was in for a long day. I was catching a 7am flight out of Newark to Tampa, Florida, for a lunch meeting in Clearwater, then heading back to Newark on a 5pm flight, getting me in around 8:10pm, and with any luck, to my apartment by 9 or so. We all have days like that, they happen from time to time.

Made my flight, everything was on time, got to my lunch meeting. Because of the training/workout schedule I'm on, my first meal of the day was that lunch. I had a healthy piece of grouper, and a very successful lunch meeting that lasted just about three hours.

By the time I got back to the airport, it was close to 4pm. Flight boarded at 4:30pm, and I knew that by the time I got home, I wouldn't have time to stop for dinner anywhere, and certainly didn't want to grab fast food at either airport.

[14] Peter Shankman. "The Greatest Customer Service Story Ever Told, Starring Morton's Steakhouse." Shankman.com. August 17, 2011. http://shankman.com/the-best-customer-service-story-ever-told-starring-mortons-steakhouse/

When I got on the plane, my stomach was rumbling a bit, and I had visions of a steak in my head.

As I've tweeted and mentioned countless times before, I'm a bit of a steak lover. I go out of my way to try steakhouses all around the world when I can, and it's one of the reasons, no doubt, that my trainer at my gym is kept in business. But it's all good—give and take. Over the past few years, I've developed an affinity for Morton's Steakhouses, and if I'm doing business in a city which has one, I'll try to schedule a dinner there if I can. I'm a frequent diner, and Morton's knows it. They have a spectacular Customer Relations Management system in place, as well as a spectacular social media team, and they know when I call from my mobile number who I am, and that I eat at their restaurants regularly. Never underestimate the value of a good CRM system.

Back to my flight. As we were about to take off, I jokingly tweeted the following:

@petershankman
Peter Shankman ✓

Hey @Mortons - can you meet me at newark airport with a porterhouse when I land in two hours? K, thanks. :)

Let's understand: I was joking. I had absolutely no expectations of anything from that Tweet. It's like how we Tweet "Dear Winter, please stop, love Peter," or something similar.

I shut off my phone and we took off.

Two and a half hours later, we landed at EWR. The fact that a flight got into EWR on time during summer thunderstorm season is a miracle in itself, but that's not important right now.

Walking off the plane, I headed towards the area where the drivers wait, as my assistant Meagan had reserved me a car home.

Looking for my driver, I saw my name, waved to him, and started walking to the door of EWR, like I'd done hundreds of times before.

"Um, Mr. Shankman," he said.

I turned around.

"There's a surprise for you here."

I turned to see that the driver was standing next to someone else, who I just assumed was another driver he was talking to. Then I noticed the "someone else" was in a tuxedo.

And he was carrying a Morton's bag.

Now understand... I'm a born-and-raised New York City kid. It takes a lot to surprise me. A LOT. I see celebrities on the Subway. I see movies being shot outside my apartment, and fake gunfire from any given CSI show, five days a week. I'm immune to surprises.

Except when they're like this.

Alex, from Morton's Hackensack walks up to me, introduces himself, and hands me a bag. He proceeds to tell me that he'd heard I was hungry, and inside is a 24 oz. Porterhouse steak, an order of Colossal Shrimp, a side of potatoes, one of Morton's famous round things of bread, two napkins, and silverware.

He hands me the bag.

I. Was. Floored. (Shankman includes a picture of him and a waiter, in full black tie, giving him the Morton's bag.

Let's make sure we're clear on a few things here…

1) I was joking in my Tweet. I never, ever expected anything to come of it other than a few giggles.

2) Morton's Hackensack is 23.5 miles away from EWR, according to Google Maps. That meant that in just under three hours, someone at Morton's Corporate had to see my tweet, get authorization to do this stunt, get in touch with Morton's Hackensack, and place the order. Then Morton's Hackensack had to cook the order, get it boxed up, and get a server to *get in his car*, and drive to Newark Airport (never an easy task, no matter *where* you're coming from) then, (and this is the part the continues to blow me away,) while all this was happening, track down my flight, where I was landing, and be there when I walked out of security!

Are you taking this all in? Because it happened to me, and I still can't even fathom it.

Think about all the things that could have gone wrong: My flight could have been delayed or diverted. I could have exited out a different location. (Had I taken the AirTrain and not had a driver, I never would have even exited that way!) I could have just missed him all together, I could have landed early, etc., etc.…

I have no doubt that countless companies think like that. They think along the lines of "Oh, too many logistics. That'll never work," and they leave it at that.

But what if it *does work?* What if it happens, and it works *perfectly,* and it shocks the living hell out of the person they do it to? Like it did tonight?

And what if that person's first thought is to make it public? Like I did tonight?

We live in a world where everyone you meet is a broadcaster. Look around. Think of all your friends, all your colleagues. Do you know *anyone* anymore who *doesn't* have a camera in their phone, or anyone who *doesn't* have a Facebook or Twitter account?

As I say in my book over and over again, customer service is no longer about telling people how great you are. It's about producing amazing moments in time, and letting those moments become the focal point of how amazing you are, told not by you, but by the customer who you thrilled. They tell their friends, and the trust level goes up at a factor of a thousand. Think about it: Who do you trust more? An advertisement or a friend telling you how awesome something is?

Of course, I immediately tweeted out what happened:

@petershankman
Peter Shankman ✔

Oh. My. God. I don't believe it. @mortons showed up at EWR WITH A PORTERHOUSE!
lockerz.com/s/130578715 # OMFG!

And sure enough, Twitter lit up like a bottle rocket. Click the image to expand it, it's worth reading.

kirstin_g Kirstin G
@petershankman no joke! That truly is outstanding!! Makes me
want to go to @mortons that's for certain!
26 minutes ago

stephaniegmack Stephanie Mack
Wow. @petershankman tweets @Mortons w/request for steak on
arrival and they actually deliver...to the airport
lockerz.com/s/130578715
28 minutes ago

divahound Shannon Huppin
@petershankman @mortons PHENOMENAL customer service!
Way to go above and beyond, Mortons.
28 minutes ago

rachellaber Rachel Laber
Love it! "@petershankman: Oh. My. God. I don't believe it.
@mortons showed up at EWR WITH A PORTERHOUSE!
lockerz.com/s/130578715 # OMFG!"
30 minutes ago

rivkaht rivkaht
Amazing RT @petershankman: Possibly the greatest #custserv
story ever, and I swear was in no way staged. Thank you,
@Mortons. I'm blown away
30 minutes ago

MsWZ MsWZ
I love it! Thank you for sharing @petershankman -- ::applause:: to
you @mortons ;)

When I got home, I actually looked inside the bag at
what Morton's gave me, and again, was blown away (here
Shankman gives a picture of the full dinner provided by
Morton's.)

And as to be expected, the food was amazing.

Of course, there immediately came a few tweets from
the other side of the camp, specifically calling out that I
have over 100k Twitter followers, and if I didn't, this never
would have happened:

@laurahvogel
Laura Vogel

"@petershankman tweeted @Mortons:
meet me at #EWR w/steak & THEY DID"
<--What if he didnt have 10K followers?
#custserv best w/out glory!

1 hour ago via TweetDeck ☆ Favorite ⏎ Retweet ↩ Reply

But you know what? I don't think that's the case. I don't think it's about my follower numbers. I think it's about Morton's knowing I'm a good customer, who frequents their establishments regularly. If you look at their Twitter stream, Morton's is known for always being on the ball, thanking those who mention they're eating there. Just a recent few tweets from Morton's proves this:

56 Mortons MortonsTheSteakhouse
Cheers! RT @huneybb: Mortons The Steakhouse was awesome last night!
5 hours ago

56 Mortons MortonsTheSteakhouse
Cheers! RT @alyonmix1073: Mortons happy hour! yfrog.com/h8msxbrj
5 hours ago

56 Mortons MortonsTheSteakhouse
Cheers! RT @mrjohner: Just woke up in middle of night and ate a piece of cheesecake I got from Mortons and a baked potato, not in that order
5 hours ago

56 Mortons MortonsTheSteakhouse
@dabulsteve We look forward to your visit! Cheers!
5 hours ago

So I don't think the number of Twitter followers I have played a big (if any) part in this story.

Shankman continues on with his lessons of why this was amazing. We're going to take what he said and expand on it.

So, what can we learn from Shankman's unexpected visit from a Morton's waiter? A number of things:

One—people will talk about the amazing things you do for them. Sadly, we live in a world where there is still a dearth of customer service, so when you go out of your way to do something good or nice or helpful for a client, they're probably going to comment on it. By the way, that's how this kind of customer service has to work. It would have seemed self-aggrandizing if Morton's tweeted about what they did. The person who is the recipient of the customer service *has* to act as your ambassador, letting people know about your good works (which is actually as traditional PR as you can get.).

Two—stay on top of what people are saying about you. Respond accordingly. If someone raves about you, a polite "thank you," is appropriate, not an invitation to get on the social media stage and broadcast all the amazing things you do.

Three—Perhaps most importantly, have a chain of command in place that actually *lets* you give amazing customer service in real time. As Shankman pointed out, had Morton's had to get permission to make this happen, at 5:10pm on a Wednesday night, there's no way it ever would have.

The other very important point about this customer service experience is that while these types of opportunities for amazing and thoughtful surprises have always been available to businesses when they heard about a good customer who wanted something, it's never been able to be done at this speed. Because of the instant nature of social media communication, this elaborate surprise was planned and executed within three hours. Additionally, Peter Shankman then wrote about the event and posted his blog that same night. This story went viral and has been viewed by countless number of people. Well played, Morton's. Well played.

Speed is the Key

Consumers are expecting better, faster customer service and social media is one way we can provide that to them. As we saw above, a number of large corporations are now using Twitter to spot, identify and resolve customer service issues. Here is a more common example of what consumers can expect from businesses on social media.

One day Nadeem's son was having problem with his Xbox video game console and asked his dad to help him fix it. After trying for a long time Nadeem was unable to fix it. He tweeted about his frustration and within minutes, an expert from Microsoft tweeted him a link to print a shipping label for FedEx. The unit was picked up the next day, and was fixed and delivered back to his happy son in 2 days all without calling an 800 number, waiting on hold, explaining the issue and trying to troubleshoot! Nadeem's family was blown away by that 'WOW' service level from Microsoft via Twitter.

Imagine you or your Agency being able to provide that level of service to your clients. With social media, it is possible. If you and your clients are connected on Twitter or other networks, you will be able to spot customer service questions and resolve them with lightning speed. Let's give them something to Tweet about!

Making Yourself Available

Providing excellent customer service doesn't always have to be extreme like Morton's Steakhouse or even Microsoft. It can be as simple as being available to connect with clients on their preferred method of communication.

Take a look at this conversation between Angela and a client:

Here's another example of using social media to connect in a manner that is convenient for the client.

One of Nadeem's clients was in Germany and was in process of renting a vehicle. He had a quick question about whether he should purchase the insurance coverage being offered by the rental car company. Knowing how active Nadeem is on Facebook and not having a way to easily call from Germany to Houston, the client sent a Facebook message to Nadeem. He received it instantly in Houston at 10:30 p.m. Nadeem was able to answer the question without hesitation and the client got an instant reply while at the rental car counter. This was such a delightful experience for the client that when he returned to Houston he sent a thank you email praising the quick service he received.

Many customer service questions, no matter how small, are time sensitive to clients. They expect an answer or response in minutes or hours, not days.

We can also hear what some of you are saying. "I can't be constantly connected to my PC or smartphone. I can't be constantly checking all of my social media networks for questions." The good news is this is not necessary. Rest assured you can remain connected and still have a life!

Most social media platforms have the options to set alerts and notifications. To be sure questions are answered in a timely manner, just make sure those alerts are set up to let you know when someone has sent you a message or mentioned your name in a comment. By doing this, you can make sure you don't miss an interaction with a client or prospect who is reaching out to you.

Setting Notifications on Your Facebook Page

Take a look at your notification settings on Facebook by going to your Facebook business page. Click on Edit Page and then Manage Notifications.

Once on the notifications screen, make your desired selections and click Save Changes. This is the place where you can tell Facebook to alert you by email and/or on Facebook when someone posts, comments or messages your page.

Setting Notifications on Your Twitter Account

To set up mobile and email notifications for your Twitter account, login to Twitter and click on the Gear icon in the top right corner, then select Settings. There are two screens you will need to look through to set all available notifications: mobile and email notifications (see below).

A nice feature of Twitter mobile notifications is that they offer sleep settings. This allows you to set on and off times for Twitter updates being sent to your phone.

Setting Notifications on Your LinkedIn Profile

To set notifications on LinkedIn, login to your LinkedIn account and click on the down arrow next to your name in the top right corner. Click on Settings from the drop down menu.

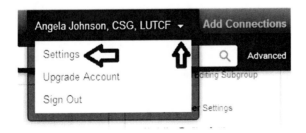

Select Communications from the menu. From there, click on each option on the right and make your desired notifications.

For the large majority of requests that occur outside of business hours it isn't necessary to drop everything, login to your system and start working. All that is usually required is to acknowledge the question and let the person know that you have seen it and will get back to them with an answer. Also, set a reasonable timeframe based on the urgency of the request.

If someone is asking for a quote on their health insurance on a Saturday for a policy that is renewing three months from now, it is perfectly fine to let them know you will be contacting them on Monday for more information. Thank them for thinking of you, make a note to call them on Monday, and go on about your day.

Sometimes issues are time sensitive or at least need to be addressed quickly if a client is upset, just like we already do when reading emails after hours. Some things just can't wait, or if the client does have to wait, they will be very upset by the time you make time to deal with their request. In those situations just follow your normal service procedures by either making contact or resolving the issue immediately.

Setting alerts on your social media site allows you to handle the emergencies which then become those precious "WOW" experiences that your customers can then let their networks know about.

Turning Bad into Good

Social media can also let you know when a client is about ready to give up and you can "save the day" and turn a potentially bad customer experience into a decent one.

Angela used Twitter to reach out to American Express as a last resort when she was approaching "very frustrated customer" status. Here's what happened.

"I'm not one to use credit cards and I stay away from opening any credit cards, regardless of the promotion or benefits. If I can't pay cash I don't get it. However, I have many clients who ask me if they can pay their insurance policies with their American Express card every year because they want to get their "points". These clients have told me about all of the great benefits they receive from American Express. This has been going on for years, but my curiosity was finally peaked when speaking with another insurance agent who went into more detail about the benefits she's received from using her American Express card.

Like magic, one day a salesperson for American Express came into my office unannounced and asked if she could set an appointment for one day next week to talk with me about the AmEx cards. One of my team members got my approval and set the appointment.

When this salesperson came in the following week for our scheduled appointment, she was professional, not pushy, gave a quick pitch about the benefits and walked me through how many points I could earn by putting most of my monthly personal and business expenses onto this card and then paying it off each month. Since my daughter was almost finished with college, thereby freeing up lots of money each month for me to start traveling to exotic locations soon (!), I was sitting in my office imagining my new jet set lifestyle. By the time my daughter was out of college I would have so many AmEx points I would travel the world in luxury for the rest of my life. Or something like that…

Anyway, I signed up for a card and my husband and I committed to putting everything on the card that we could. I was especially excited about the ability to earn TRIPLE points when booking travel through the American Express web site because I had a lot of business travel coming up that would rack up those points even faster for my world travels. When the cards came I created my online account and went to work converting everything to be paid by American Express.

Imagine my delight when the dates of my next travel plans were announced. I could finally earn those triple points by booking the travel through the American Express website (see you soon, Paris!) But when I logged in to the travel portion of my profile I got an error message. After trying different ways to access it online, I called the 800#. You know the drill. I waited on hold forever, explained the issue, the lady told me to reboot the pc (not really, but it was something as equally ineffective) and said that since I was a new member she needed to have that portion of my account set-up. I have blocked out the exact details of what she and the other four or five people I talked to said, but the issue was never resolved. I explained the problem to many AmEx representatives, sent email screen shots to people trying to assist, and tried different things they recommended with no success. I got an email back saying the problem had been corrected, but when I tried to login and book travel it still didn't work. Grrrrrrr. I replied back to the email, letting the representative know it still wasn't working, but got no response back. Ever.

I even reached out to the lovely lady who opened the card for me. After several days she told me her supervisor was going to escalate the issue and she would get back with me right away. Six months later and I'm still waiting to hear from her, but I digress.

Don't get me wrong—American Express has great customer service. They were all very polite and seemed to really be trying to help me, but I had truly tried everything I could think of and was ready to cancel the card. To heck with the points!

This was an issue no one had seen before; they escalated to Tier 2 and tried all kinds of things on my account. I was finally offered the solution of making my travel reservations by phone with American Express so I happily called the phone number I was provided, but was very unhappy to find there was a fee to use that service. But, the *points*! The *triple points*! So I agreed to the fee, booked my travel, and earned my precious points.

Since my card was brand new, and since I truly don't believe in or need a credit card, I was ready to cancel the entire card. After all, if I can't book my own travel without paying a fee, why even have the dumb card, regardless of the points?

The following week I had another trip that I needed to book travel reservations for, and in a final act of desperation, I tweeted to American Express, giving them one last chance to fix my online travel booking issue. Within a few minutes I had a tweet in response letting me know they received my tweet and would send me a message to get more details. Someone immediately sent me a direct message via Twitter, identifying herself as the single point of contact for my issue from now on. She provided me her direct email address and asked me to send a screen shot of the error message. We went back and forth in email a few times and my problem was resolved that day.

If American Express had not had someone monitoring their Twitter account who responded to my tweet, I was going to cancel my card the next day. It was going to be a reasonable amount of trouble to convert from paying with cash or a debit card for everything and moving to American Express anyway. And there was no reason to spend the time I didn't have on making that fundamental switch if I really couldn't even get the thing I was most excited about: *Triple Travel Points.*

I most definitely was ready to cancel the card, and I definitely would have tweeted a few more times about how frustrated I was with American Express, how much time I invested in trying to fix this problem and how no one was responding to me.

But this story has a different ending, all because one person took a few minutes to make a personal connection and help me. My account is set up correctly and I am happily earning single, double and triple points for my purchases. And when I get enough of them stocked up, Greece, here I come!

The moral of this story: stay tuned to what your clients are needing and wanting. However, because many of you probably are connected to large carriers, pay close attention to when your clients are having issues with the parent company. They might not let you know about it but will say something about it on their networks. If you are connected to your clients via social media, you will get that feed and you'll be able to address their concerns quickly and personally.

Robot Social Media = Bad Customer Service

There is another example of a customer service issue that went really wrong, really fast because an insurance company chose not to make a personal connection but instead set up "robot" tweets to respond to inquiries about a negative story that was going viral.

In August, 2012 a story hit the media about Progressive. Not only did television news pick up the story, so did social media users who angrily reposted, retweeted and discussed the details online.

In response, Progressive set up robot tweets that repeated the same message over and over again instead of responding to each tweet in which they were mentioned. This made them come across to the public as an uncaring, unfeeling corporation, which is exactly the opposite of the image they're portraying in their ads.

The moral of this story: By not paying attention to what was being said on social media, Progressive had a PR disaster they had to deal with. So do be careful of what you post and how you respond to what others post about you. Progressive is large and can absorb the enormous hit they took with that story. As individual agents, we probably wouldn't be so lucky.

NOTE: For more information on the details of this story, you can Google 'Progressive robot tweets' and choose an article from the many results your search will return.

The Personal Touch

It can seem counterintuitive to think people expect a personal touch from social media, since that contact is not face to face, or even voice to voice. However, consumers are using social media to communicate personal information with their friends and family. When they (as a person) add, follow or fan us as a business entity, they are expecting to be met with good customer service with a personal touch. The Morton's Steakhouse and Progressive examples are a good lesson for those who don't yet believe that Internet connections are real.

8 Improve Retention and Cross Sales

> *"In the world of Internet Customer Service, it's important to remember your competitor is only one mouse click away."*
>
> —Doug Warner

WE'VE ALL HEARD THE STATISTICS: IT COSTS FIVE TO SEVEN times more to obtain a new customer than it does to keep an existing one. It is no secret the insurance industry has one of the highest new customer acquisition costs. As we pointed out in Chapter Six, Angela spent $167 per new client when she was only using direct mail marketing.

There are many reasons people become insurance agents. We want to make sure our clients are protected and we want to help them stay safe. However, let's also be honest. This is a business, which means we also are in the business to make money, and agents quickly learn that the "bread and butter" of this business isn't new clients, but the money that comes from renewals.

Renewals are to insurance agents what summers are to teachers. Now, we're not suggesting that some agents get into the insurance business just for the promise of renewals, or that some teachers decide on their profession just so they can have summers off, but these sure are nice perks to the job!

Renewal commissions provide the cushion we can rely on for a break. After the first five years of putting our blinders on, heads down and building our agencies, working day and night, weekdays and weekends, renewals are the light at the end of the tunnel!

Good renewal numbers of course mean that your customer retention numbers are high. When business is retained, the opportunities to increase the total number of policies per household through cross-selling increases as well.

The importance of retention and cross-selling reverberate throughout our businesses. Without a good retention ratio most of us would lose appointment agreements with our carriers, jeopardizing our entire livelihood. In this "insurance as a commodity" world we are headed towards, the more policies a client has with us the less likely they are to leave. That's why the number-of-policies per household is also such an important number. As the number of policies per household increase, so does the likelihood they will stay with our agencies longer. These two agency measurements are inter-related: The higher our cross-sale ratio, the higher our retention rate and the happier we'll all be.

Good, caring customer service is the backbone of high retention and cross-selling rates, and that kind of customer service comes with genuine engagement. From an agent's point of view, an engaged client means a client who is not lost in the filing cabinet or database after a sale is made. It means a new contact or client is aware of our products and services and is ready to connect with our agency as soon as his or her needs change or a new need arises.

From a client's point of view, an engaged agent is someone who takes the time to connect with him or her, who knows something more than just how many cars the client owns or what the deductible on their health insurance is. According to MDRT research, an average insurance client expects an agent to connect with them ten to twelve times per year. That means an engaged agent is someone who is in touch and interested in the client beyond just what they can be sold.

When the agent is engaged and providing superior customer service, the client will feel more inclined to stay with their agent, even if a better deal presents itself. They'll be more willing to call the agent for more of their insurance needs, and (looking to the next chapter), they will feel comfortable referring their friends and family to their agent. That is invaluable to any business person, including an insurance agent.

Here's the bad news: aside from collecting premiums, the industry average for client "touches" is paltry. An agency barely connects with each client one to two times a year. Part of the reason for this is because until the rise of social media there hasn't been a good opportunity to personally connect with a client ten to twelve times per year that wasn't overwhelming and time consuming for Agents and intrusive or annoying for clients.

We could send a birthday card, maybe a Thanksgiving or Christmas card, leave a voicemail asking to get together for an annual review or mail out a quarterly newsletter. But think about what we've talked about throughout the book so far—the importance of engaged reciprocal communication. The communication in all of these traditional examples are only one-way.

Moreover, in a not-so-funny irony, our success as agents mean that the bigger our book of business grows, the less likely we as the agent probably answer the phone or take payments. This puts us back to square one, struggling to connect with clients.

Until social media, the best way to connect with a client was to talk with them when they called in with a question or dropped by to make a payment.

Social Media Improves Customer Retention

Did you know that "reducing customer defections by as little as 2% per year is equivalent to cutting costs by over 10 percent?" Or how about the fact that "a sustained 5 percent improvement in an insurance agency's customer retention rate can double profits in five years?"[15] As business owners, these are the kinds of numbers that can make or break our agencies in the long run.

When Angela's friend had her figure out how much she was spending on acquiring new clients, she decided

---

[15] Lynn Thomas. "Customer Loyalty and Retention Primer." Roughnotes.com. www.roughnotes.com/rnmagazine/search/management/98_02P60.HTM. January 27, 2013.

to cut back on mailing and focus more on retention and cross-selling by utilizing social media. She liked the price (free!), and she had been using it successfully to connect with friends anyway.

As we talked about in Chapter Three, it's important to upload contacts into your social media networks and start making connections. This includes friends, family and yes, even clients. So that's what Angela did. She connected with clients on Facebook and LinkedIn and went to work.

When final results for 2012 were posted Angela looked at her retention numbers versus last year to see if she could pinpoint any specific results to social media. For 2011 her retention ratio was 6.37 percent better than the state average in her company. For 2012 her retention ratio was 16.36 percent better than the state average in her company. Not too shabby! She had a 10 percent gain in retention year over year, during a very volatile year rate wise, going from 85.39 percent for 2011 to 95.07 percent retention for 2012. How much money in your pocket would a 10 percent boost in retention equate to?

To maintain a good retention rate, agents used to call each client around renewal time thanking them for their business. When an agency begins to grow and an agent's office gets busy, this is often one of the first things to be eliminated because it is time consuming. Additionally, in today's society most people aren't home to answer the phone during the day and don't want to take such calls in the evening.

Social media is a perfect way to bridge this gap! It is convenient for clients because they are already spending time on social media and will gladly connect with you there. It is easy for the Agent because one message goes out to all of your prospects, clients, contacts, and centers of influence (those major referral sources you work hard to acquire and maintain) all at the same time.

Getting Past the Transactional Relationship

By genuinely connecting with clients using social media we are able to deepen our client connections past the transactional relationship.

Through social media, clients are able to watch our agencies grow and progress. In this way, we build trust with them. Social media also allows us to stay current in their lives but in an unobtrusive way. This furthers the trust and commitment between both agent and client, which is a true win-win.

Here's an example. A couple of years ago, Nadeem was doing a policy review with a client over lunch and they added each other as friends on Facebook. Just recently, this same client called Nadeem with an insurance question. When the client called, instead of asking him generic routine questions like, "How is your family?" and "How do you like this weather?" Nadeem was able to jump in directly with the question about a trip to Alaska that the client recently took. Because of their Facebook connection Nadeem was able to see pictures of the client bicycling through Alaska. Nadeem was able to connect with the client at a deeper level when he asked the client specific questions about his trip. The client loved this and was more willing to take Nadeem's advice about the insurance that he needed.

When we as insurance agents connect with clients at this level, they no longer look at us as regular vendors who are trying to sell them something. They look at us as a trusted friend and professional who understands their needs. This is the power of social media in action.

By connecting with our clients via social media, we as agents are adding personal-touch service to our clients. That personal-touch service is the exact reason insurance companies choose to use agents as their distribution system instead of choosing to use a direct writer. Social media is the next logical place to take our agencies to enhance this all important personal service.

Gentle reminder: As we've talked about, it's not a good idea to make people feel stalked on Facebook. That's exactly how people feel when someone comments on or "likes" *everything* they say. However, social media is there for us to be social, so look for conversations that interest you and contribute to them. Facebook is a great place to give recognition for anniversaries, birthdays, weddings, births and other special events. That is, however, not the time to try to cross-sell something. Just stop in and leave a natural, genuine Congratulations note and be on your way.

By engaging with clients through platforms like Facebook and LinkedIn, we are given the opportunity to increase our likability factor. There aren't many, if any, clients who look forward to paying their insurance bill. How many times have we all had a client come to the office to pay their bill(s) and jokingly say something like, "Well there goes all my money!" And with insurance they get nothing specific to show for all that money until that dreaded day when disaster strikes and it was all worth it. However, that disaster may be twenty years away. In the meantime we want to be perceived as a friendly place to do business.

Building Customer Loyalty

According to Ethan Block, existing clients have reduced price sensitivity and reduced switching to competitors.[16] Loyal, existing clients also give more referrals and cross-sales. On the other hand, new customers require the cost of acquiring them through advertising and marketing, they require more of your time to make the initial sale and then set up their new account, and they are more price sensitive until they become a loyal customer.

The key is to shorten the time it takes your new clients to become a loyal customer. Social media represents a great way to position ourselves as likable, friendly and knowledgeable. It's a great avenue to introduce and feature the talents of your staff as well.

We have mentioned the importance of including your staff in your social media campaign. As agency owners, you can't grow your business if you are answering the phones and sending out new Auto ID cards or updating commercial insurance certificates. You must have staff to help with those tasks, and your clients have to get to know and trust that staff. Social media is a great way to help that process occur faster.

Take the opportunity to feature not only your overall agency accomplishments on your social media networks,

---

[16] Ethan Block. Flowtown.com. "The Value of an Existing Customer." October 17, 2010. www.flowtown.com/blog/the-value-ofan-existing-customer#ixzz12k1JvufP. January 20, 2013.

but also those of your individual team members as well. It's great to post commendations, milestones and accomplishments of staff and congratulate them publicly on your business Facebook page. Here's an example of one of Angela's team members:

Staff members should also add items of importance to their LinkedIn page so everyone can see that your staff is just as professional as we the agents are.

By featuring your staff in this way, clients who are connecting with you on social media will be less likely to get upset if he or she cannot speak with you on an issue. They will be comfortable with a team member helping them when you have positioned your staff as valuable and knowledgeable.

By giving us the ability to listen and respond quickly, social media offers the upper hand in providing the all-important WOW customer service, which improves retention. Studies show that just because a client is satisfied doesn't mean they will be a loyal customer. People in general expect to be satisfied when they spend money with a business. It is the WOW customer service that will really have an impact on retention.

This isn't always something that can be provided in every transaction or encounter with a client, but when the opportunity arises, you have to take advantage of it. Social media enables you to respond to your clients in a totally effective way.

For instance, at Christmastime 2012 Nadeem received a gift basket from his landlord and he proudly posted a picture of it on his business page. One of his clients saw the post and made a comment that she wondered if she will get a basket from her insurance agent. Although she was only joking, Nadeem immediately responded by ordering a Godiva chocolate basket for her. A few days later the client received the delivery and was completely delighted. She responded by thanking the agency publicly on his Facebook page.

This client had never connected with Nadeem directly. She has 5 policies with the agency and always been a loyal client but had never reached out to make a personal connection. This channel gave her an opportunity to connect with the agent directly in a very convenient way and it gave Nadeem an opportunity to create a WOW experience. How likely do you think that client will be to stay with Nadeem, seek him out with additional insurance needs, and be willing to refer him to friends?

A Trail of Breadcrumbs to the Cross Sell

Let's get into the nuts and bolts of cross-selling via social media. Social media is a fantastic place to plant the seeds of cross-sales. It can't be said too many times: the higher the number of policies a client has, the less likely they are to leave.

There are many things you can do to cross sell on networking platforms, but before we get to those, another word of caution: Whatever you do, if a major flood wipes out an entire section of a country and hundreds of thousands of people are swept away and killed, do not put up a post about why everyone needs flood insurance. It won't go well, trust us!

It's not a good idea to come across as opportunistic at the time of someone else's misfortune. You can't set a trap and then snap it closed and make a sale. It's much more effective to leave a trail of bread crumbs and let the clients walk to your door, asking for more—more information about insurance products, more interest in having you quote additional insurance products, or simply wanting more coverage.

There are many excellent ways to do this. One method is to post articles that act as a proof source for something related to the products and services you offer. Articles written by someone else reinforce what you believe is important. For example, it is okay to repost a newspaper article about why apartment dwellers need renters insurance. This is showing that we are informed professionals who stay on top of news in our field.

However, don't use an article of an apartment fire in your neighborhood where people have been left homeless and then say they should have had renter's insurance. Do you see the difference? The first example is informative. The second example can come across as uncaring and opportunistic.

Another method is to follow insurance blogs and then post a link to a good article from that blog. Blogging is becoming ever more sophisticated, and they are a great way to find good content to share with your social media connections.

For instance, for a life insurance professional, an article with facts and figures regarding how much life insurance the average person needs would be good to share. This gets people thinking about what they need, and then encourages them to think of you when they are ready to purchase.

If you think about it, these methods are the same idea as having brochures in our offices. These brochures aren't written by you, but contain valuable information. You pass them out to clients to give them more information with your business card stapled to the front so when the client is ready to purchase this additional policy, they call you. It's the exact same concept, except online!

Another method to drive cross-sales is by posting about unique or specific benefits your products offer that others in the industry don't.

And one more caution here—a caution that we've already talked about when we told you about Angela's gaff trying to pivot a sale when she learned about the motorcycle crash. It's actually called Life Event Marketing. This is what we call the act of watching your social media friends and then pouncing when they have a life event and offering to sell them something. When someone brings a baby home from the hospital they only want to hear words of congratulations. While they may be thinking of their need for more life insurance and will contact you soon, they don't want you to comment on their babies pictures and ask what the child will do if they (the parents) die in an accident in the near future.

This is an extreme example, but we hope it makes our point. As sales professionals, be careful to use social media to deepen connections and pull them to you, not push people away. Although we may know "Mr. Jones" has no life insurance and his family will lose everything within a month if he suddenly dies, a public forum isn't the place to make that sales pitch. Remember: Lay out a trail of bread crumbs and let people come to you.

Tra*digital* Retention

It's a nasty world out there with many people trying to lure away your hard-earned clients. The need to continually connect to your current client base is perennial. Traditional marketing methods leave a lot to be desired because, at the end of the day, the client can see through the phone call that came right before the policy was up for renewal. Retention ratios are boosted because you can now connect with clients in meaningful ways. Even though it is a digital format, never forget that online conversations can lead to offline connections, and vice versa—which is how the world communicates in the twenty-first century!

Here's just one of thousands of examples of this happening. It comes from Renee Corwin-Rey's Facebook page. This agent received a message from a happy client who had received a call from her office and posted about it. The offline phone conversation resulted in online engagement from an existing client who gave the agency not only a happy testimonial, but a strengthened relationship with endless possibilities. Here's the simple exchange:

So a few minutes ago, I got a call from Heidi, thanking me for being a customer of Corwin-Rey Insurance Agency! I want to thank YOU guys for being so dedicated to great customer service, and for constantly reaching out to your clients, to remind us how important we are to your business-- simply awesome :)

Like · Comment · January 18 at 4:17pm near Centralia, WA

 Lisa Buchheit likes this.

Corwin-Rey Insurance Agency Thank you, Thank you, Thank you...Yes it was fun calling as many of our clients we could get ahold of today just to say THANK YOU.

January 18 at 5:44pm · Like · 1

When clients know and trust you, then changing carriers becomes a much more complex decision. This is exactly where we want your agencies to be, and it can happen so much more effectively when connections happen in real time in the digital world.

Gain Referrals

> "Word-of-mouth marketing isn't about giving customers talking points, as if they were brand spokespeople. It's about delivering an exceptional customer experience that makes customers want to recommend you."
>
> —Deborah Eastman,
> "Clearing the Air About Word-of-Mouth"

WORD OF MOUTH HAS ALWAYS BEEN THE MOST EFFECTIVE way to gain new business. That is simply because people trust what their friends, family, or trusted professional tell them. It's the reason why a "center of influence" is so valued. They refer business to the agency on a continual basis, and they do so because they trust that their hard-earned clients will be well taken care of.

Referrals are the best present anyone could ever give a business person. It means that the agency has taken a person from being a customer, to a client, to an advocate. Referrals are far easier to close than any other kind of prospect and thus do not have the high acquisition cost of other customers. They tie up all of the keys to a successful business into a neat little box. The client is saying, "I did business with you, I enjoyed that experience, I'm going to continue doing business with you and I trust that you will treat my friends and family well also."

Referrals come because our customer service is stellar, because we have done our job right.

The Power of Social Media

Referrals are going to happen with or without social media, but as the tra*digital* model has taught us again and again, social media can facilitate the referral process and amplify it exponentially. It isn't just a person-to-person format that happens, but a person to multiple-person platform that allows a message to be amplified.

Your clients can and will tell *your* story on *their* social media networks. This is going to happen whether you have a business presence online or not. If a consumer has a really good experience or a really bad one with your agency, just because you don't have a Facebook page does not stop them from using Facebook to tell their friends about that experience. It just keeps you from being able to listen and respond to that experience via the method the client prefers to communicate.

The referral process works in this way on social media. It offers marketing opportunities to reach not only clients and friends that we are connected with, but also the networks of those friends. On each platform, when someone interacts with your page or content, their friends are able to see what they liked or commented on. This frequently generates curiosity and those friends then visit your page to see what is going on. Provided you have a well-cared for page with interesting content, they are likely to begin following your page simply because they trust their friend's judgment.

Here's an example of how this worked on Angela's network. Her twenty-one year old daughter, Aricka, was surfing the internet one day and came across a blog post titled, "An Open Letter to the Fat Girl I Saw at Hot Yoga in New York City."[17] In it the author hilariously but in the end poignantly talks about how she saw another "fat girl" doing hot yoga at her studio in New York City. The author never met the girl, and it becomes a sort of paen to women everywhere who fight against the cultural push to be thin and finding a way to love their bodies in spite of it all. The blog post goes from talking about how the author found herself, "easing back into my Fat Down Dog, forward to Fat Plank, then melting and pushing up to Fat Cobra, etc. etc., all the way through my big fat hot Vinyasa flow," to admiring the other "fat girl..putting your big ol' ass into yoga pants." The author eventually moves into how angry she is with her body but has come to be "nice to it anyway, three times a week at Hot Yoga," to finally applauding the other "fat girl at hot yoga," with "You are trying to find a way to be stronger, to live in yourself, to like your body enough to give it that seventy-five minutes of movement and acceptance. To just take care of the damn thing, even if you ARE mad at it. To treat it like an exasperating, ugly, ill-tempered little child—one you secretly adore."

---

[17] Joshilyn Jackson. "An Open Letter to the Fat Girl I Saw at Hot Yoga in New York City." Faster than Kudzu. December 29, 2011. http://www.joshilynjackson.com/ftk/?p=1675

Aricka thought this post was so endearing and funny that it made her want to try hot yoga. She was away at college and searched for a nearby hot yoga studio. Since it was a small college town, there weren't any hot yoga studios.

Undeterred, she did a Google search for hot yoga studios near home, back in Friendswood, TX. She stumbled upon Pearland Bikram Yoga and because they are socially connected, she was able to check out their web site, Facebook page, Yelp and Twitter accounts.

The next time she came home, she asked Angela to go try Bikram yoga with her. Angela went, almost died (but loved the challenge of mind over matter) and a new addiction was born for both of them. The studio owner, Taz, happened to be the instructor in their first class. Taz made the whole experience so positive and interesting that they both started going to class regularly and posting about their Bikram yoga adventures on social media.

This is where it gets interesting from a referral standpoint. Since they started talking about Bikram yoga on social media, there are now at least twenty people who have tried Bikram yoga and many of those have gone to the same studio Angela and her daughter frequent. And now those people have told *their* friends how much *they* love it, and now *their* friends are giving Bikram yoga a try.

That's a lot of referrals considering Bikram yoga is not very well known, especially in Texas where it is already hot enough without working out in a 105 degree room, and is very intense and challenging. This kind of yoga is not like recommending someone go try a new candy bar. There are investments to be made in clothing and mats, and the class costs money and each class lasts ninety minutes.

Even with these barriers to entry, Angela and Aricka have ended up directly referring a number of people who then referred their friends to Bikram yoga simply by stating how much they enjoy it on their social media networks—all because Aricka was bored one day and was surfing the 'net. That's some powerful stuff.

Referral Gone Bad

When customer service goes south, of course there go your referrals. And this can get especially scary when you are connected to a large corporation. Think back to the Progressive PR nightmare. Think about what could have happened if the insurance company in question wasn't a direct writer.

There is an interesting phenomenon that happens on social media. It has to do with the amplification aspect we mentioned above. You've heard of the term "going viral?" It's when something sweeps across the internet—a story, a funny picture, a new game, a video. It's what we love to see happen when the product of interest is ours. But going viral can have its negative side too, and because it usually has to do with very bad customer service, you know it can't be good for the referral game.

The best example of this is the story that went viral about the airline carrier who threw around a musicians' guitar and then wouldn't pay for the damages. The guy whose guitar got damaged, Dave Carroll, first wrote a song about it and made a video out of the song that he posted on YouTube.

The song went viral, and became so popular that Carroll even wrote a book about it. The saga is yet another tale of horrible customer service that turned into a PR nightmare that the airline handled very badly. And in a strange twist, Carroll is now an internationally acclaimed speaker on the importance of customer service. You can read all about it by Googling "United Breaks Guitars."

According to Wikipedia, here's the response from the United Breaks Guitars YouTube video: The YouTube video was posted on July 6. It amassed 150,000 views within one day, prompting United to contact Carroll saying it hoped to right the wrong.[5] The video garnered over half a million hits by July 9,[7] 5 million by mid-August 2009,[4] and 10 million by February 2011.[18]

The fallout has been nothing short of amazing. Taylor Guitars gave Carroll two new (very expensive) guitars. He's been on all sorts of media from CNN to Jimmy Kimmell, and in January 2013, the success of Carroll's online protest was used by the German television and news service Tagesschau to exemplify a new kind of threat facing corporations in the internet age.

The "threat" is that with social media, people no longer are powerless against powerful entities with a lot of money to fight legal battles. The battles are now played out on the internet, the social equalizer, but that door can swing both ways. We applaud it when it works in our favor, we groan when it doesn't. But at the end of the day, it all comes down to good customer service. If United bought Carroll a new guitar and maybe threw in a travel voucher for good

[18] "United Breaks Guitars." http://en.wikipedia.org/wiki/United_Breaks_Guitars

measure, that would have played out far differently on social media in a very positive way for United, and people would consider switching their airline of choice to United instead of away from them.

The Hip Referral Gathering Place

The effectiveness of this one video shows the reach and power social media has on the decisions of not just your own networks, but the networks of your networks, and so on.

This has even farther reaching implications for insurance. According to Bazarrvoice.com, *44 percent* of Millennials say they would not purchase insurance without referencing others' opinions.[19]

Millennials are those born from the late 1970's to early 2000's. They have been raised with increasing levels of technology and feel very comfortable online. We would even venture to say that if this group can't easily find and interact with agencies online, they will find someone else to buy insurance from.

Facebook, ever the leader in trends, came up with a way to facilitate this new development in buying habits of their customers. They created "Graph Search" which makes it easier than ever to see what businesses your friends approve of (i.e. "Like") without even having to ask them. This takes the idea of "referral" to a whole new level.

It works like this: when doing a search for "Insurance Agent" in Billings, Montana, Facebook will pull up agents who have indicated they are located in Billings, Montana.

---

[19] http://www.bazaarvoice.com/research-and-insight/social-commerce-statistics/#.UZ_5YrWsh8G

However, the results will be ordered according to how many of your friends "like" each page. The agent who more of your friends also like will appear first on the list, and so on. If none of your friends "like" the business page of an insurance agent in Billings, Montana then Graph Search uses other data to determine the order, such as which page has the most overall page "likes".

In general, people like to stay together as a group and take action as a group. It's just human nature. We can all probably point to groups of people in our own books of business who are all connected and referred by each other. Maybe it's a family or a group of friends who one-by-one all moved their insurance to us. Maybe it's a group of people who work together or who were part of the same Greek organization at their college.

In other words, these social networks are simply the twenty-first century version of the age-old phenomenon of the "tribe."

The "Tribe" Phenomenon

Seth Godin, the guru of internet marketing, wrote a book about it called, simply, *Tribes*.

He asserts that people have always congregated into groups that have the same interests, beliefs, goals—you name it and there's probably a group formed around it.[20]

Back before mass media, our group or "tribe" held a very powerful influence over us. If the group liked it, we liked it. If we liked something but it was frowned upon by the group, we might have had to go along because if we didn't, we'd get kicked out of the tribe and have to make it on our own.

---

[20] Godin, Seth. Tribes: We Need You To Lead Us. 2008. Print.

Social media has basically brought back a "tribal" mentality into our consciousness. The millenials look to what their "friends" are doing online. Social media networks have allowed this natural tendency to group together on like-minded beliefs and desires by creating groups and forums. People want to be part of something, part of a community of like-minded individuals. And so naturally when someone in their community says "my insurance agent is great!" the rest of the people will at least show interest if not follow the lead outright.

And what's most interesting about groups, now and in the past, is that there have always been individuals whose opinions matter more than others in the group. These are the group leaders, but they don't necessarily have to be the named "leader." These are the people who are worth taking time to identify and befriend because their recommendation carries more weight than most of the others in the group. That's a traditional tip that you can easily apply to your social media marketing campaign, but we digress.

Insurance agents who are getting measurable results from social media are doing so because they have created a community of people who share in their same interests, goals or dreams. Their fans and followers are able to relate to the agent as a person and they like what they see. Success on social media can't be attained by begging people to purchase insurance. It has to be earned by creating a real connection with folks.

We can't stress this fact enough—it's the real connection between people that prospects, customers, and clients want and expect online. That connection can be made in thousands of different ways. Nadeem frequently uses his social media networks to post inspirational quotes.

These quotes generate questions and discussions that Nadeem moderates, asking more questions and encouraging opportunities for his fans to interact with each other and connect. The people he attracts are the people who like inspirational quotes and all the other things Nadeem is interested in and talks about on his social networks. He is a huge fan of Tony Robbins—he's even done the firewalk. Nadeem also is a Jim Rohn fan, and so he posts Rohn's ideas and quotes which then generate discussion on his page.

Most important, none of Nadeem's comments are forced or fake. He just started posting thoughtful quotes about topics that interested him by people whom he admires. He is being his authentic self, and like-minded individuals enjoy being a fan of his social media networks. They also enjoy doing business with someone who thinks like they do.

Food trucks build like-minded communities really well. Since food trucks are, well, mobile, the only way to find out where they will be parked each day is to follow their social media sites. That is kind of the fun and uniqueness of food trucks! Their food is consistent and reliable, but their location can be a mystery. If you want to eat their food you have to wait for their location announcements and hope it is convenient for you. Not everyone enjoys this unpredictability. Only those who see themselves as self-proclaimed "foodies" will go to the trouble of hunting down food served out of a truck. And that's how the food truck community, or tribe, has been created.

As insurance agents, it may take a little creativity when developing a sense of community. A bakery, for example, has a much easier time creating an online community because they can post pictures of their beautiful pies or cakes or cupcakes. Their natural market is people who like sweets, and isn't that almost everyone?

Since we don't have a tangible, attractive product to take pictures of, we have to think outside the box and focus on a creative aspect of insurance, such as protecting one's family.

To make the "tribe" idea work for you, give some thought to ideas or items you are naturally interested in and work that into a common theme on your social media networks. Write them down and figure out ways you can get other like-minded people involved in conversation about it. You'll be amazed at the referrals you can make from this one activity.

Centers of Influence

We have spent the entire book talking mostly about connecting with individuals. We have mentioned the importance of centers of influence earlier in the chapter, and we want to take a moment and discuss how social media can enhance that very important relationship.

Centers of influence have traditionally come from making connections person to person. We meet a realtor or mortgage broker, we find that we share business ethics, and we start referring business back and forth.

When social media is used effectively, we are able to target people who can be key referral sources for our business. Realtors, mortgage brokers, CPA's and bankers are also building their social media presence, and this mutual desire to provide a good referral source to each other's respective clients provides a unique opportunity to connect with them. In short, they're looking for the exact same thing we are—leads. Of course, the best way to *get* a referral is to *give* a referral, like the one below.

 Angela Johnson-Farmers Insurance shared Amanda Borham-Hernandez, Keller Williams Realtor's photo.
May 1

Looking to buy or sell a home, rental or investment property in West Houston? Amanda Borham-Hernandez, Keller Williams Realtor can help. Call her today!

When we are connected with these professionals and engage them on an ongoing basis, they feel comfortable and will refer business to us. In return we promote them and their business, and now this type of relationship can be done completely online. Social media keeps the dialogue going and creates opportunities for a strong business relationship. It is also much less time-consuming and usually far more consistent than face to face visits weekly.

If you are a P&C Agent like us, it's very likely you were advised to go around to apartment complexes and car dealerships to develop centers of influence. You may have been taught to take in a box of donuts to the office staff or sales team and make friends with them so they would send you referrals. This may work for a time.

However, as an agency starts to grow it becomes more and more difficult to get around to these places at least once every week or two, so most agents slowly stop going. When they stop making the rounds on a frequent, consistent basis, the referrals stop coming.

For a center of influence to continue to provide leads, you have to stay in front of them as a reminder that you are available to service their clients. As soon as you slip, there is another Agent ready to replace you. That's what makes social media so brilliant. It is an efficient way to constantly stay in front of your centers of influence. By connecting with office staff and salespeople online, you are able to make contact with them daily if desired.

But it's not only "making contact." You are able to remain in touch with them, commenting on pictures of their kids and pets and reading about what's going on in their life each day. They will be doing the same for you. Although we will still need to make face-to-face contact regularly, a little more time can pass between office visits than before, and when you do see these folks you will be able to have more meaningful conversations.

The value in all this? When another agent tries to woo them away it won't work. You are now their legitimate friend, both online and IRL (in real life) and they will not be open to referring business to another agent as long as you continue to nurture that friendship.

When social media is used effectively, you are able to target people who can be key referral sources for your business.

10 Humanize Your Agency Brand

"A brand that captures your mind gains behavior.
A brand that captures your heart gains commitment."

—Scott Talgo

THINK ABOUT HOW MANY AGENTS THERE ARE WHO SELL the exact same product you do. Five thousand, ten thousand, twenty thousand? More?

That's a lot of internal competition. How do you differentiate yourself from the agent who offices in the next strip mall over and represents the same corporate brand? The same way you've always done it. You make it personal.

The idea of a "brand," is actually a large corporate type concept. "McDonalds" is a brand. You know what the golden arches are all about, and whether you like the food or think it's the worst stuff on the planet, you know what you're going to get when you walk in a McDonalds.

Here's an interesting experiment. Walk into three different McDonalds. It's going to smell the same and the colors are all going to be the same—that's part of the corporate brand—but the feel of each of those three restaurants are going to be different. That's what we mean by an agency brand. One McDonald's that Angela visits greets their customers by saying, "What can I make for you today?" It feels like they are actually making the food fresh and care about taking care of their customers. That's a very different message than the McDonald's that says, "Can I take your order?" That subtle message relays that the employees are order takers serving up frozen food.

As we've said before, insurance coverage is an intangible product but it is critical to the financial and asset protection of our clients. In order to do our job most effectively, it is imperative that we are viewed as a trusted professional. The policies and coverages we suggest to clients are things people hope they will never need. Not having proper coverage when the worst occurs can be financially devastating.

Still, insurance coverages are one of the first places to be cut when money gets tight, so our clients need to trust that they can rely on us for professional coverage suggestions and advice that will protect their families and assets.

If there is one thing that social media can accomplish in spades, it's humanizing our agency brand. What that means is simply, as an agent, we have a brand, something that makes us different than the thousands of other insurance agents under each corporate umbrella. That's the "agency brand" part. When you "humanize" it, you're literally putting a human face to your business—yours. Social media provides the opportunity to humanize your business like no other form of marketing has ever done.

When you've humanized your agency brand, your social media network begins to see you as an insurance professional offering a product they value instead of a faceless person who collects their insurance premiums every month. This potential shift in a clients' perception of you shouldn't be underestimated.

Insurance is usually the last thing people like to discuss—or at least in a positive way. But by humanizing your business, clients can see that insurance isn't so useless, scary or even boring.

Highlight Community Activities

We've talked a lot about posting interesting personal content interspersed with information about insurance. One way to show a personal side of your business is to highlight community activities and causes you support.

For example, Angela is a big supporter of March of Dimes. Most people today are familiar with March of Dimes and their fight to end premature births. But Angela supports them for a different, more personal reason. Her grandfather was a polio survivor who was left a quadriplegic in 1952 as a result of the illness. It is the research spearheaded by March of Dimes that sped up the vaccine development and saved countless others from the devastating effects of polio. Although the vaccine was developed after it was too late to save him from a life of paralysis, March of Dimes provided her grandparents with help and resources during the early years after he contracted polio.

Each year Angela has a team that participates in the March for Babies walk in Houston, and of course she posts about it, before, during, and after the event.

Community involvement is nothing new, but in the past it was more difficult to get the word out about causes we support. In the era of social media, everything from the beginning to end of a campaign season can be orchestrated online. From recruiting team members, soliciting for donations and wrapping it all up with pictures of the event and a final tally of money raised, social media allows us to tell a full story from A to Z.

Even though the insurance company we represent may be big and faceless, our agencies are run by real people who contribute to our communities. This separates us from the herd and helps to make us the logical choice when someone is searching for a new agent.

When people see that you won an award for being an exceptional agent, or have been honored because of some volunteer work you've done, they feel assured that their business is being taken care of by a competent agent and it reinforces their belief in your agency and keeps their confidence high. This of course results in all those things we desire as agents: new business, higher retention numbers, and all the benefits that come with that.

Take for example insurance agent Joel McKinnon. He posted on Facebook about a sign that he saw at a baseball field titled, "He's Just a Little Boy," by Chaplain Bob Fox. It's a great poem that really gets to the heart of a little boy who is at bat, misses a pitch, and finds the game "is no longer fun." The poem asks us to remember "he is just a little boy," and have compassion on him.

McKinnon saw the poem printed on a poster at a baseball game. He liked it so much he ordered several of the signs and started putting them around the ball fields in the city where he lives. When he posted about the sign on Facebook it created a wonderful effect. It really touched his audience and people started supporting it. The post had nothing to do with insurance, but because he took the time to actually do this and found a way to post it without being self-aggrandizing, it resulted in very high engagement with his client base. It gathered some other benefits too. He was published in an MLB publication and was mentioned on an Atlanta radio station. This built a lot of credibility for him among his existing clients, it got his name in front of a lot of people, and it showed everyone on Facebook an agent who cares.

There are lots of ways to humanize your agency brand. For example, post a funny or touching YouTube video. Make sure to fill out all the honors, awards, and educational information on Linked In. Talk about the volunteer work you do on your Facebook page. Tweet about something you're in the middle of that would be of interest.

Imagine you are a client who has received an auto insurance quote from two different agents. One takes some information and quotes you the 6 month premium over the phone. The other one sends an email with the quote information and they also refer you to their LinkedIn page for more information about themselves and their agency. When you simply click through to their LinkedIn page and view their profile you see a list of Honors, Awards, Education and Professional Recommendations from other clients. Which Agent would you be more likely to choose?

If there is a great story behind something you've done, share it. People love stories, especially real stories of real people. Anyone can go online and get a quick quote for most types of insurance. But those quote generators aren't a person. You are! Use that to your full advantage.

Be a Successful Tra*digital* Agent

Social media is an amazing tool. It can handle so many aspects of traditional sales and marketing that it's almost mind boggling to think about!

Social media gets everyone involved. It's one big beautiful conversation, and tapping into that communication stream can be a powerful tool to help you grow your business.

We hope you also really "get" that social media can never completely replace traditional marketing. You will always take a box of donuts to property management companies, send direct-mail, and attend networking events. But this can all be enhanced by social media.

Because we've given you a lot of information, we're going to end with a traditional recap, a few key reminders for becoming a successful Tra*digital* Agent:

1. Your clients are online. They need to be able to easily find you there, too.

2. To get good results from social media marketing, you must use it consistently, just as you would any marketing tool.

3. Social media marketing shouldn't be the only thing you do to market—it's meant to be an additional tool in your marketing toolbox.

4. There isn't a "set it and forget it" method that will get good results with social media. Remember to engage with people and be social.

5. Work strategically—systematically allocate time for each network and have specific goals that you monitor for yourself and your staff.

6. Use all channels in concert—think of each component like a musical instrument and it is when they are all deployed in an orchestrated manner, the full strength of the spectrum can be experienced and effective results can be achieved. You have to use multiple social media tools to capture all the benefits.

7. Set correct expectations for your social media results.

8. Keep the information on social media profiles updated and current.

9. Most important of all, have *fun* with it! Be your genuine self. Allow yourself to make mistakes, laugh at yourself when you do, cry and commiserate with others, rejoice in their triumphs, and invite them to rejoice in yours.

Social media is still very much a new frontier, and it will always remain so because it will continue to change as fast as it was created. But know this: At its heart, it's people connecting with people. And no matter how many ways in which you do that, the byproduct—happy clients who continue to do business with you—will always remain the same.

Postscript:
Enhance Traditional Marketing
With Digital Weapons

"How can you squander even one more day not taking advantage of the greatest shifts of our generation? How dare you settle for less when the world has made it so easy for you to be remarkable?"

—Seth Godin

WE HOPE *GOING TRADIGITAL* ENCAPSULATES THE IDEA FOR you that whatever marketing methods you can do offline can easily be done online as well. Who knows what will happen tomorrow, but in today's world, the most effective marketing strategy consists of both traditional and digital methods.

Instead of ending with some grand concluding statement about how everyone needs to be online, we want to acknowledge something as equally important in today's marketplace. We all have clients and prospects who either like to do business in a completely traditional or completely digital manner. There are also a set of consumers who utilize both methods.

In order to capture the most business possible, agents have to be available offline *and* online.

So to end, here's a list of ideas on how to combine Traditional and Digital Marketing to get you started as a Tra*digital* Agent!

DIRECT MAIL

On your traditional marketing letter or postcard, add a QR code directing prospects and clients to your web site or Facebook page. You should also include your web site, blog, business Facebook page or other online address where prospects can find more information about you online.

NEWSLETTERS

Rather than mailing out a monthly or quarterly newsletter, start an eNewsletter. You'll save money on postage while also creating content that your Social network can share with others! You can also use those same eNewsletter articles as blog posts. If you must mail out hard copy newsletters, be sure to add a line for your web site, Facebook or other Social Media address.

ANNUAL REVIEWS

A great alternative to face-to-face annual reviews for your busy clients is using Skype or a G+ hangout. This allows you to have a "face-to-face" time with the client in a more convenient way. When preparing for client account reviews, check out their LinkedIn profile for any change in needs for insurance or financial services products that come from job changes.

MAIL/EMAIL

On your company letterhead, add a line for your web site, Facebook or other Social Media address. In your email auto-signature, include a link to your web site, Facebook or other Social Media address. Many Agents use their email auto-signature to list out products they sell. Why not link to your blog where clients can read about these products and see that you are a competent professional who offers a suite of different products?

BUSINESS CARDS

Update your traditional business cards to include your web site, blog, business Facebook page or other online address. It's also a good idea to add a QR code to the front or back of your business card to direct people to your online presence.

QUOTING

When presenting a proposal, direct prospects and clients to your LinkedIn profile. This will give them the opportunity to do some research on your agency and strengthen your professional value proposition, making you a more logical choice.

YELLOW PAGES

Make sure your business listing in the yellow pages will also be included in their online directory. This way you can maximize your advertising dollars to catch clients both offline and online. It's also a good idea to create a company G+ page and fill in all of your business information completely. This will boost your business up higher in Google search results when a prospect is searching for insurance locally.

CHAMBER OF COMMERCE/BNI NETWORKING

You should still continue networking in person if that is working for you, but also take your networking one step further and connect with them on your social media networks. This will give your contacts the opportunity to see your successes and information about the products and services you offer more frequently and provide you more opportunities for touch-points.

APARTMENT COMPLEXES/AUTO DEALERSHIPS/ REAL ESTATE RELATED VISITS

If you're a P&C agent who visits apartment complexes to write more renters policies, visits auto dealerships to write more auto policies or realtors, title companies and mortgage offices to write more home policies, connect with these sales people on your social media networks. This will deepen your relationship and keep you top of mind when their clients are looking for an agent.

BILLBOARDS/BUS BENCHES

Add your web site, Facebook page or other online address to your existing billboards and bus benches so that people who want to connect online can easily find you.

DOOR HANGERS/WINDSHIELD FLYERS

On your traditional door hangers and windshield flyers be sure to include your web site, blog, business Facebook page or other online address where prospects can find more information about you.

COMMUNITY BULLETINS/DIRECTORIES/ NEWSLETERS/NEWSPAPER INSERTS

When advertising in Community newsletters or newspapers be sure to include your online contact information along with your traditional phone number and address.

TELEPHONE COLD-CALLING/DOOR TO DOOR MARKETING

When utilizing cold calling or door to door marketing for businesses, use your online resources before making the call or visit. Social media sites like LinkedIn and Facebook make great resources for information on businesses. Use social media information and intel in reverse to gather facts and data. Striking up a conversation about a unique aspect of the business will set you apart from all the other unsolicited marketers they are used to brushing off.

RADIO AND TV COMMERCIALS

At the end of your commercial be sure to tell people where they can find more information or contact you online. Consider having your Twitter hashtag in the bottom corner of the TV commercial and telling listeners what your hashtag is during your radio commercial.

PROJECT 100 LETTERS

When first starting in the insurance business, we were all told to make a Top 100 list of contacts and mail them a letter introducing our new career choice. In addition to sending out letters to your Top 100 contacts, import that same list into Facebook and LinkedIn and connect with them online as well.

BIRTHDAY CARDS AND OTHER ACKNOWLEDGEMENTS

Facebook is an easy way to quickly leave a personal note for your connections. Whether it is a birthday, birth of a child, a wedding or a host of other life events, simply posting a comment on someone's Facebook page is an acceptable and effective way to let them know you're thinking about them.

RECRUITING ACTIVITY

When looking for new staff members, announce the opening on your social media networks. On Facebook, create an ad to promote the post about the job opening. Target users within a certain radius of the job location zip code. However, don't limit this ad by keywords because you want everyone to be able to see the ad. This way your friends and fans that may not be qualified for the job will still know about your job opening and can refer any good candidates they know of to you.

AFFINITY MARKETING

Use the Advanced Search feature on LinkedIn to find those with keywords, specific titles, industries or companies listed in their profile. You can narrow your search by location and then connect with prospects as appropriate.

CAR SHOWS/HOME IMPROVEMENT SHOWS/ HEALTH FAIRS USING FISHBOWL DRAWING

Offer participants an extra entry for the drawing if they become a fan of your Facebook page.

PROMOTIONAL GIVEAWAYS/CALENDARS/PENS

Be sure to include your web site, blog, business Facebook page or other online address where prospects can find more information about you.

Appendix A:
Tools to Simplify Social
Media Marketing

GOING TRADIGITAL HAS ONE GOAL IN MIND: TO HELP YOU understand that what people need and want from an insurance agent will never change, but the way we connect to our potential and existing clients has changed, and it is vital for the success of our businesses to use social media effectively.

However, we have only just scratched the surface of all the tools available on the Web to help manage your social media campaign and keep it from consuming your day.

The following are tools that we have found very helpful to keep us focused on what's important so we don't get sucked into the social media abyss (and it can happen, trust us.).

Not all the tools are specifically social media-related. There are other online tools that can help when you're ready to go to the next level of internet marketing, such as how to set up and successfully run a blog. There are tools listed that are specific to insurance agents. They are listed in alphabetical order so you can find them easily.

There is plenty of business out there for all agents to make a good living. We want you to be as successful as you want to be. Just like with any other aspect of social media, try these tools out and see which ones work best for you!

About.me

This is a free service that lets you consolidate all social media contact information in one place. You can think of this as a business card for your social media addresses. Once you register your name with about.me, you add information about yourself and links to all your social media channels. That way you can use this one link for directing everyone to all your channels. You can use your about.me address in your email signature or on your business cards.

To sign up for this service go to www.about.me.

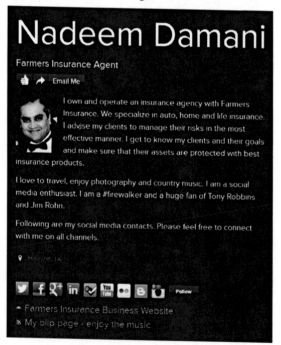

Blogs

A blog is an excellent way to raise your name higher in Google search results. By blogging about popular topics that your target audience often searches for, Google will see your blog as a more and more relevant place to send users. This is a critical component of an effective inbound marketing strategy to drive people to your web site. You should post a new blog at least once per week.

It's also really important to have a way to capture email addresses of those who visit your blog so that you can market to them later. Be sure to have a way for them to subscribe to your blog so you can get an email address to add to your database.

Blogging can be set up at many sites. Two of the most popular are http://www.wordpress.com or http://www.blogger.com.

WordPress is web software you can use to create a beautiful website or blog. The core software is built by hundreds of community volunteers. There are thousands of plugins and themes available to transform your site into almost anything you can imagine. Having a good website is essential to capture leads that you may generate from social media. If you already have a company website, you can maximize the features that help you customize it and if you decide to create your own blog or website, you can consider using WordPress to do so.

Blogger is a free service provided by Google and an easy way to start your own blog. You can sign up for this using your Gmail log in and start blogging in minutes. It is very simple to use and also lets you use various designs and templates.

ConnectMogul

ConnectMogul helps agents leverage their book of business and connect via text messaging with their prospects and customers. Agents using this system have been able to write more policies and increase efficiency in 10 'beginning of day' processes. This makes you more money. This makes you a mogul. **Over 97% of people open their text. Over 93% of people read their text within 2 minutes.** Register for this service at http://www.goingtradigital.com.

connectmogul helps agents leverage their book of business and connect via text messaging with their prospects and customers. Agents using our system have been able to write more policies and increase efficiency in 10 beginning of day processes. This makes you more money. This makes you a mogul.

Over 97% of people open their text.

Over 93% of people read their text within 2 minutes.

Features

Prospect
Prospect x-date tracking
Automatic text to prospect
Upsell
Bundle up sell texts
Retain
Birthday texts
Appointment reminders
Bill reminders

Constant Contact

Constant Contact is a leading provider of e-Newsletter services. They offer various plans for different size mailing lists. This service is ideal for running your own e-newsletter campaigns. You simply import your various email contacts (think clients, prospects and x-dates) and can then send monthly or quarterly newsletters. This is also an ideal service to promote events that your agency may be holding for clients.

Constant Contact is also becoming more integrated with social media. They have an app you can install on your Facebook business page that encourages your followers to join your email mailing list as well as a service called Social Campaigns.

For more information go to www.constantcontact.com.

Going Tra*digital* Subscription

A web-based subscription to the Going Tra*digital* online content is a great way to stay current on everything new and improved in the Social Media world. Through blogs, interviews and how-to videos we share tips, tricks and ideas to keep your Social Media usage profitable, relevant and current.

Register at http://www.goingtra*digital*.com/.

Hootsuite

As we discussed earlier, Twitter is one of the best platforms to meet new prospects and offers tremendous opportunities to connect with centers of influence. However, there is so much information that flows through Twitter that it can be overwhelming.

That is where Hootsuite comes in. With this free service, you can divide all the incoming information into separate channels and look at it from different angles. You can make groups and look at information coming in from certain groups. For example, you may want to build relationships with local Realtors so you form a group called 'Los Angeles Realtors' and create a stream under Hootsuite. This stream will allow you to look at tweets that are being posted by members of that group. Or you can form a group of all your clients that are active on Twitter and you can monitor what your clients are tweeting about. Using Hootsuite streams makes it easy to engage with your target audience.

Besides Twitter, Hootsuite also supports other channels like LinkedIn and Facebook so you can have all different streams under one platform. This way, if you want to post content to multiple channels, you can easily do it with Hootsuite.

To learn more about Hootsuite or to sign up, visit www. Hootsuite.com.

iWowwe

This is a service that can be used to send video to one or multiple recipients. It is said that if a picture is worth a thousand words, then a video is priceless. This service allows you to make quick videos to communicate with your clients and has ability to direct the viewers to a specific web site at the end of the video.

For example, you can send new clients a Welcome video. At the end of the clip they'll be automatically directed to your Facebook page so they can "like" your page and stay connected.

For more information, visit http://www.iwowwe.com.

Job Change Notifier

Job Change Notifier is a free service that sends you an email alert when one of your LinkedIn connections changes jobs. This is advertised by Job Change Notifier as allowing you to stay up to date on your professional network.

In insurance sales, timely information is vital in making sure we get in front of the right people at the right time. The information can be used to build relationships by contacting those who may have a change in needs for insurance and financial services products.

For more information, visit www.jobchangenotifier.com.

ManageFlitter

This service helps you continue to grow your Twitter account by managing your followers. Once you are following over 2000 people, Twitter puts a restriction on the number of people you can follow. When you reach 2000 followers, you can only follow up to 2200 users. In order to keep growing your connections, it becomes important that you unfollow people who are not active on Twitter, those who may be a fake account or those not following you back. ManageFlitter quickly analyzes all your connections and breaks them down into categories so you can decide who to unfollow. We recommend logging into ManageFlitter once a month and cleaning up your Twitter followers so you can keep growing your Twitter account.

This is a free service and can be found at www.manageflitter.com.

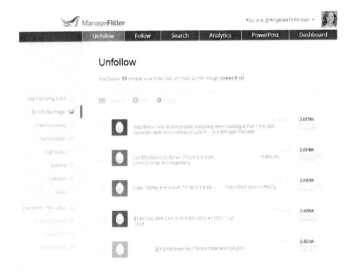

My eSig

Name, email, website, mobile number. It's all right there at the bottom of your email, but does anyone even notice? Transform your boring, outdated email signature into clickable, interactive buttons that drive people to your website. Your buttons are completely customizable, and you can link them to anything on the web, including your website, online store, Facebook, Twitter, Linked In, resume and videos! My eSig's easy-to-use design tool gives you full control over your email signature, change fonts, colors, sizes and more. Set up your new email signature quickly, and you can change it whenever you want! With the number of emails flying back and forth these days, you're way too interesting to be another victim of the scroll-through phenomenon. Make your emails stand-out with eSig!

For more information, visit http://www.myesig.com.

Pagemodo

This service helps you design a professional, custom Facebook page for free. Pagemodo offers customizable templates and custom tab images, a cover photo editor, apps for fan coupons, contact forms, maps and more.

For more information, visit http://www.pagemodo.com.

PODS

For tracking sales and marketing activities in general and social media activities in particular, this service is a must. PODS is a web based service that allows you to track all the activities you or your staff members are engaged in, in terms of sales process and service work.

For example, you can set an activity to go on social media and connect with 3 new realtors per day. Once you have that goal set in this software, it will track your progress on a daily or weekly basis. This can help you manage your time more effectively, especially when using social media for marketing.

To sign up, please visit http://www.goingtradigital.com.

QR Code Reader and Creator

To download a QR Code Reader to your smartphone, go to the AppStore and search for the term QR Code Reader and select one to download.

To find a QR Code Creator, search for the term "Free QR Code Creator" in your internet browser and select one. Most are very user-friendly. Simply enter the URL you want to send users to and click "Create". Then you can save the QR code as an image and insert it into marketing letters, promotional materials, business cards and much more.

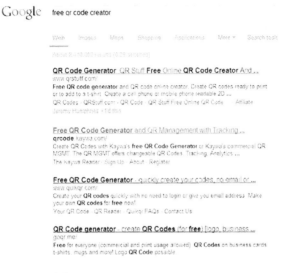

Tweetadder

This service adds a whole new component to Twitter by giving you the ability to automate some parts of your daily Twitter activity. For instance, this service lets you schedule posts on a recurring basis and that way you stay active active on Twitter. Because of the volume of content posted on Twitter, tweets are pushed to the bottom of the screen very fast. In order for your messages to be seen, it makes sense to repeat it on a regular interval for maximum impact. Tweetadder allows you to do this automatically.

Another great feature of TweetAdder is that it automates following several hundred contacts automatically during any day. It allows you to follow targeted contacts in your area by setting it up to follow those who follow local businesses or professionals on Twitter. For example, in order to find local Twitter users who would be interested in your products and services, you simply tell TweetAdder to start a following those users who follow local TV or radio stations. Soon you will be following tons of new contacts in your area who you can engage with and in turn many will follow you back.

Sign up at: http://bit.ly/WIX61d.

Wildfire

Promotions are a proven way to grow a social audience, engage consumers and drive sales. This service can help you rapidly create and deploy your promotion with ease across multiple social networks, including Facebook, Twitter, LinkedIn and YouTube. Run any kind of promotion—contests, sweepstakes, coupons, giveaways, and others—and track the results in real time. Watch your audience and sales grow.

Create and launch any type of promotion that fits your business objective. This service also provides the ability to track the effectiveness of your promotions by providing additional information and analytics.

For more information, visit http://www.wildfireapp.com/products/promotions.

Websites

The following are good places to start for developing your website if you don't already have one. Because this is a book on social media, we did not delve into this topic, but do know that they are important in this new age of internet marketing.

Websites are where you send people for more information. They're a landing page that can sell your services directly or capture email addresses to be added to your newsletter campaign. We recommend you find a professional website company who knows how to integrate blogging, landing or squeeze pages, SEO and drip email campaigns so that all online efforts are working in concert together to turn your agency into an inbound marketing machine.

Hubspot (www.hubspot.com) is a company that puts this all together into one package. There are many more companies to choose from, so do a search and start interviewing a few until you find the best fit for you and your budget. Just remember, you get what you pay for! It will take lots of research and training to develop a web site that generates results on your own, so you'll have to weigh what your time is worth versus the cost of paying a professional.

Here are some sites you can use to set up a website on your own:

http://www.wordpress.com or http://godaddy.com or http://www.networksolutions.com.

New tools and services are always being developed. You can find our most current list at http://www.goingtradigital.com.

About the Authors

 **Nadeem Damani** graduated from the University of Texas in 1993 with a BBA in Marketing. He has been an Insurance Agent with Farmers Insurance since 2002. His agency is located in Stafford, Texas. His accomplishments and awards include seven-time Championship designation, eleven-time Topper Club attendee and one time Million Dollar Round Table qualification. In 2005, Nadeem Damani was number one in the company out of 16,000 Agents in writing term life policies. Damani has been actively using Social Media for the last four years to build his insurance business. He speaks at various company events regarding his Social Media strategy. He has over 40,000 connections in various Social Media networks including Twitter, Facebook and G+.

Angela Johnson obtained a BA in Literature in 1996 from University of Houston-Clear Lake. After working in mid-level management with a major phone company, she started her career as a Farmers Insurance Agent. Angela started a scratch agency in 2005 and currently has 3,800 PIF. She has achieved Topper Club and Championship multiple times and is a member of Presidents Council. Angela has been honored to address her fellow Agents at many events including Town Hall, Topper Club, South Texas Mega Conferences and many social media seminars around the country. Although she began using Social Media solely to keep tabs on her daughter, she quickly embraced it as a way to build relationships with long lost friends and then as a way to make new ones.

CPSIA information can be obtained
at www.ICGtesting.com
Printed in the USA
FSOW01n1841030415
6132FS